Offensive Conduct
MY LIFE ON THE LINE

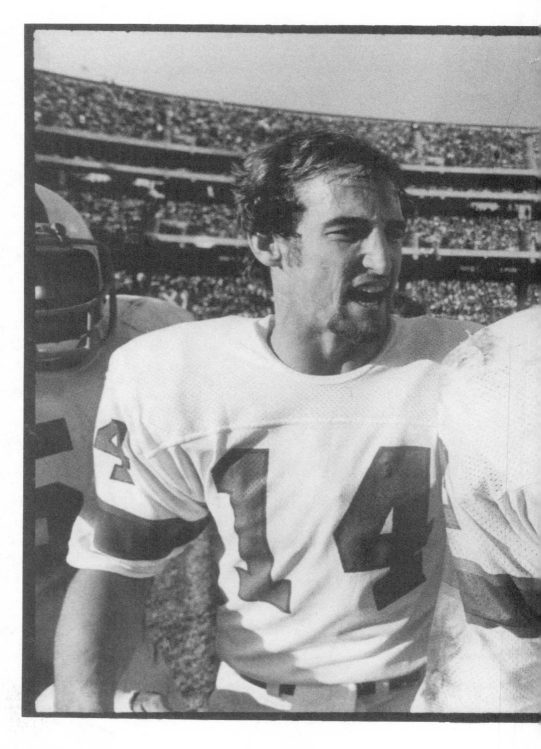

Offensive Conduct

MY LIFE ON THE LINE

John "Hog" Hannah with Tom Hale

TRIUMPH
BOOKS

Library of Congress Cataloging-in-Publication Data
Hannah, John, 1951-
    Offensive conduct: My Life on the Line / John Hannah with Tom Hale.
    pages cm
    ISBN 978-1-60078-860-4 (hardback)
    1. Hannah, John, 1951- 2. Football players—United States—Biography.
    I. Hale, Tom, 1957- II. Title.
    GV939.H28A3 2013
    796.332092—dc23
    [B]
                                2013013262

This book is available in quantity at special discounts for your group or organization. For further information, contact:
    Triumph Books LLC
    814 North Franklin Street
    Chicago, Illinois 60610
    (312) 939-3330
    www.triumphbooks.com

Printed in U.S.A.

ISBN: 978-1-60078-860-4

Design by James Slate

Photos courtesy of Charley Hannah and David Hannah unless otherwise indicated

Front title page photo courtesy of Getty Images

This work is dedicated to my Lord and Savior, Jesus Christ, the Son of God Almighty, who has borne my transgressions, forgiven my sins, and shed light upon my path to Eternal Life. I pray the words of my mouth and the meditations of my heart will be acceptable and pleasing in His sight. Amen.

Contents

Foreword

I WAS ALWAYS A collector of magazines, and because of my interests, *Black Belt Magazine*, *Karate Illustrated*, and *Sports Illustrated* were three of them. I remember picking up a *Sports Illustrated* in August 1981 and reading it with great interest because John Hannah was on the cover. Like me he was an Alabama native, and I had recently watched a game where he had battled tooth and nail with Randy White. The magazine proclaimed that Hannah was "The Best Offensive Lineman of All Time." I was totally fascinated and read it cover to cover.

Fast forward less than a year, and I had been drafted by the New England Patriots in the second round of the 1982 NFL Draft. Being a high draft pick at linebacker, all I could think about was: *Don't let John Hannah put you in the hospital.*

As rookies we had to report to training camp about 10 days earlier than the veterans. The anxiety for the rookie linebackers built as the veteran reporting date approached. The buzz in the locker room at Bryant College was all about John Hannah. As it turned out, we should have been even more scared than we were. Our first morning session with the veterans had all of us rethinking our strategy for the second session. Hannah went through us like a hot knife through butter and had every one of us reporting to the equipment room for horse collars and more pads to wear under our shoulder pads. By the end of the first day, we were trying to figure out how to have him kidnapped.

Hannah made us all better football players just by his presence. You knew you better "come correct" and use all of your best techniques in practice and buckle up every time he was on the field. He led by example. He was never one to give speeches, but his desire to win was obvious, and we all fed off that.

Truth be told, I never even had a conversation with John until 1986. It was my first Pro Bowl after our appearance in Super Bowl XX. Right after practice he gathered all of the Patriots Pro Bowlers together and said, "Look, Pat Sullivan gave me some money, so that we could all go out to dinner on the team. Let's meet with all our families in the lobby around 6 o'clock." I remember it like it was yesterday. There I was, a veteran and Pro Bowler, who had just played in the Super Bowl, and I was mesmerized because a guy who had been my teammate for four years was talking to me!

Of course, over time we became friends, but I never lost that level of respect for John. When you are being considered for the Pro Football Hall of Fame, the voters give a lot of weight to what your opponents and teammates say about you. John, being who he is, commands a lot of respect when he discusses the attributes of players with whom he competed. I consider it a great honor to have had John Hannah speak out on behalf of my candidacy. When I was later elected to the Hall of Fame and John said, "Welcome to the fraternity," I was almost speechless.

Having been retired from the game for almost 20 years, I have the benefit of perspective. I can honestly say that one of my proudest accomplishments is that I am in three Hall of Fames (the Pro Football Hall of Fame, the New England Patriots Hall of Fame, and the Alabama Sports Hall of Fame) with one of the greatest to ever play the game. I'm also proud to call him a friend.

As the best offensive lineman of all time, John was the ultimate protector on the field. Off the field, he is the ultimate protector of his family, his friends, and this great game of football that we all love.

—Andre Tippett
New England Patriots executive director of community affairs
Pro Football Hall of Fame Class of 2008
New England Patriots 1982–1993

Introduction

I HAVE KNOWN John Hannah and his family since 1971 and remain very close to him and his brothers, Charley and David. The Hannah name is truly legendary in the SEC, the University of Alabama, and the New England area, and John's legacy as a Pro Football Hall of Fame lineman with the New England Patriots from 1973 to 1985 is forever immortalized in the August 3, 1981 edition of *Sports Illustrated*, which summarily declared him "The Best Offensive Lineman of All Time."

I'm a few years younger than John and when I was 14 and a freshman at Baylor School in Chattanooga, Tennessee, I became aware of who John was about the same time I met his youngest brother, David. He was in my freshman class, too, and even though he was a supremely gifted athlete and I was only mediocre, we struck up a friendship that has endured and grown stronger for more than 40 years now. As close as our friendship has been, I don't necessarily find it a complete coincidence that I lost my older brother, Chip, within a couple of hours on the exact day in 2007 when David lost his oldest child, Bill.

I was also an acquaintance of the middle Hannah brother, Charley, who was also at Baylor when I was there, but we didn't become friends really until three or four years ago. A while back I reminded Charley, who had an outstanding career of his own with the Oakland Raiders and Tampa Bay Buccaneers, that my friendship with him mainly revolved around his penchant for picking me up and throwing me over his head into a corner because I was sitting in his favorite chair in the commissary or pulling me headfirst by the hair out of the antechamber of the lunchroom. (Apparently, I had it coming because I was only a sophomore.)

With all these Hannah encounters and events in my early teens, I became an instant fan of John's, even though I had only seen him in person once and had never actually met him. Before we became great friends six or seven years ago, the only time I saw him was when he walked into the dining hall at Baylor with his dad, mom, Charley, and David just after he signed with New England. The room of chattering prep boys and clattering silverware quickly silenced as everyone looked to see this awesome display of genetics appear in the room. John was a pinch over 6′3″ and 275 pounds and looked as if he had less than 10 percent body fat. He was *huge*. His shoulders were twice as wide as his waist, and his arms were thicker than my thighs. I, along with 100 other dorm students, just stared for a moment. Besides David and Charley, I'm quite certain no one else in that room had ever seen such a giant like him—let alone an NFL player.

With his additional extraordinary talents in track and field, baseball, basketball, and wrestling, John is still regarded among the best large athletes to have ever lived. Having personally seen most every professional game he played with the Patriots and witnessed many of the other superhuman feats he performed in wrestling and track, I wholeheartedly second that notion. Hannah's main acclaim, however, comes from the 13 bruising years he played with the Patriots, and in the process he earned the right to be regarded as the finest, most feared offensive lineman to have ever played the game of professional football.

If you look up the all-time highlight films of *Sports Illustrated*'s top 100 pro football players, Hannah is No. 24. The highlight clips of "the Hog" absolutely demolishing the defensive line and secondary—game after game—will leave little room for doubt that No. 73, the left guard for the Patriots, was a force never seen before and one that has never been seen since.

John Hannah was in a league of one. He was a raging bull, who could fire off the line like a cannonball. His aim was true, and the monstrous hits he put on opponents were simply brutal. Quick as a puma and with concrete legs of coiled steel, Hannah could pull and sweep right with quarterback Steve Grogan right behind him so close he kept his fingertips on John's flank. Hannah would lower his head, throw those massive arms up, and bulldoze into the defensive line and secondary, sometimes blowing out four or five guys in a single run. He would literally knock them out of the way like bowling pins, and Grogan or another back could easily pick up six or seven or more yards running behind Hog. If by chance Hannah hit the ground on the first punishing lick, replay films show him instantly springing back to his feet in full forward motion and taking out at least one or two more defenders just for good measure.

New York Jets defensive lineman Joe Klecko, who repeatedly faced Hannah and narrates the *Sports Illustrated* highlights film, called Hannah a freak of nature. He said, "Linemen aren't supposed to be that quick and mean. They're supposed to basically stand firm and let you try to muscle through their sheer body size. Hannah, however, was coming right at you like a pissed off King Kong. And boy, if he ever connected square with you, it was going to hurt like hell."

Klecko points out a particular highlight where Hannah was staring down Randy White, the fearsome defensive assassin from the Dallas Cowboys. When Hannah shot off the line, and he and

White hit each other full speed, all 6'7" and 275 pounds of the Dallas defender was literally lifted off the ground and hurled backward. The great Randy White ate most ordinary linemen for lunch and then spit them out. Not John Hannah.

John's explosive play on the gridiron earned him All-American honors at Alabama, nine Pro Bowl appearances with the Patriots, and enough trophies to be split between the Pro Football Hall of Fame in Canton, Ohio, the New England Patriots Hall of Fame in Foxborough, Massachusetts, and the Alabama Sports Hall of Fame in Birmingham.

This is a brutally honest book; John calls it a "book of revelation." He said, "People may not believe it, but that monster I was on the playing field—and the ego that accompanied it off the field—was really just a complete charade, an act. I was nothing more than an impostor trying to play this larger-than-life super-athlete when in truth I was really this very sensitive, caring guy inside who just wanted to help people less fortunate than I was. The problem was the more I played the charade, the better I got, and I became trapped by it. I literally got taken hostage by that impostor."

I won't give it all away here, but John is truly a unique man who has not rested on his laurels and fame. He has overcome some huge personal obstacles—mainly his pride and addiction to control—to continue his life's true calling to be more than a supremely gifted athlete. His once-subordinated quest to be a convicted servant of the Lord now finds him equally at ease among princes and paupers and unashamed of the blessings that allowed him to soar to the height of fame but which also almost killed him in the process. While hiding inside a football uniform and helmet, "Hog" Hannah was blessed with superhuman athletic abilities but cursed with an inhumanly high tolerance for pain. He drove himself through coach Paul "Bear" Bryant's college powerhouse Alabama football program and took his talents to the top of professional football and beyond with only marginal regard for anyone.

From childhood Hannah's athletic achievements fed his gargantuan ego. His ungodly physique and All-American image saturated sports reports. He was idolized by fans, mere mortals were awed, and most opponents were just hurdles that stood in the way of his quest to be the best football player he could become.

But his post-NFL life became a series of humbling downfalls, including a contentious divorce from his wife and being fired as coach of his high school alma mater. Pride comes before the fall, and God used Hannah's vanity and ego against him, knocking him to his knees, and correcting him as though he was an arrogant, defiant child. At 55 years old, Hannah discovered himself in Psalm 73—appropriately the same number he wore on his jersey during his entire college and professional career—and began the first steps of his new life, free of the impostor image and gilded armor he had worn as a senseless brute.

Without question John's passion for leading others to a rich spiritual life is anchored by an indefatigable faith in the Almighty. As he has finally put the impostor in the past and in proper perspective, John no longer dishes out pain and punishment. He uses his time, platform, and name recognition to reach out to people and fulfill what he couldn't do all those years as a football player: counseling people—particularly fathers and sons who need to reconnect.

Among John's greatest leadership talents are extraordinary insight and motivation. He uses genuine humility and frankness to bring others inspiration. He is widely sought as a keynote speaker by many organizations to share the qualities, which define leadership and is regularly consulted by many companies, including the Patriots, to motivate management and build their leadership skills. John Schnatter, the CEO and founder of Papa John's, asked Hannah to deliver the prayer before the start of the 2009 Papa John's Bowl, and the words Hannah spoke from his heart to 100,000 fans are testament to the extraordinary character of a man and former football star, who still touches thousands of people every year through his enthusiastic, unshakable faith.

As John has transitioned away from football and the impostor he struggled with, he is now known by many people as a football legend, successful financial advisor, father, brother, uncle, fundraiser, coach, motivational strategist, loyal friend, and a witness to God's grace. I simply know him as a friend I call "Brother." Over the last four years, he has transformed from the greatest football idol I ever had to one of my best friends. I am much better for his friendship, and it is an extraordinary privilege to share his story with you. John has climbed with me to loftier heights of spiritual awareness than I ever imagined possible, and the ascent has ironically led to a deeper, richer understanding of where the holy spirit dwells in all of God's children who seek Him.

—Thomas S. Hale, Esq.

CHAPTER 1

Lessons from the Bear

IT WAS A long way from Albertville, Alabama, to Boston, Massachusetts, home of the New England Patriots. For a young country guy who got his start as an All-American guard in the SEC, it was also a long time from 1973 until I retired in 1985. Coach Paul "Bear" Bryant, the legendary, larger-than-life head football coach for whom I played at the University of Alabama from 1969 to 1972 would one day call me "the best offensive lineman I ever coached," a quote I would also laugh about much later as being the furthest thing from the truth of how he really felt about me. In fact just before the '73 draft, Bryant told me privately I wasn't good enough to turn pro and simply dismissed my request for some guidance.

With the new eyes I have now, eyes that God has opened, I realize maybe his quote was a way of motivating or possibly even apologizing to me—instead of capitalizing on the fame I would earn playing professional football, which I thought he did for so many years. I hope I'm right. If I'm not, or in either event, I forgive him completely for not believing in me and encouraging me when I needed it most.

Coach Bryant always carried a poem in his wallet titled "This Is the Beginning of a New Day." If he ever told anybody why he carried it for so many years, I don't remember, but here is how it read:

> This is the beginning of a new day.
> God has given me this day to use as I will.
> I can waste it or use it for good.
> What I do today is very important, because
> I am exchanging a day of my life for it.
> When tomorrow comes, this day will be gone
>   forever,
> Leaving something in its place I have traded for it.
> I want it to be a gain, not a loss—good, not evil.
> Success, not failure in order that
> I shall not forget the price I have paid for it
>
> —W. HEARTSILL WILSON

The author, Heartsill Wilson, was an accountant in Texas who also worked on the sales staff of Chrysler. Considered one of the finest sales consultants to the automotive industry, he was one of the most respected motivational speakers of his time.

One of the greatest gifts Wilson had, which I now believe probably appealed most to Coach Bryant, was his ability to see the best in people and get them to see their own value and talents. His philosophy of leadership was often referred to as "peopleology," a term loosely defined as the art of seeing things from someone else's perspective, and in the world of sales, his mantra was "to sell Jim Brown what Jim Brown buys and see Jim Brown's needs through Jim Brown's eyes."

I also personally think now that Coach Bryant carried that poem as a gut check or a reminder to balance his leadership style every now and then away from being a total dictator and a chronic, often punishing, masochistic football coach with exercising encouragement and positive praise of a player's strengths rather than constantly harping on his weaknesses. I remember one particularly grueling practice early in my playing days at Bama when Coach Bryant felt I wasn't giving my absolute best against the defense. He came down out of the tower—where he sometimes watched practice—pulled me out of the line, grabbed me by the face mask, and yanked me over to the sideline like a dog by the chain. "Hannah!" he growled, "You fat, lazy turd! You're better 'n that, boy! You better dig real deep and find out who you are in the gut, boy—in the gut—because I ain't seeing anything but a fat, lazy turd, you understand?" This rebuke out in front of the rest of the squad scared the complete life out of me. I stood there, huffing and heaving and tried to nod my head. "Hannah," he continued, "you better find out who you are, boy, and find out if you're really as good as you think you are. You got a lot of promise, boy, and if you want to play for me, you gotta show me who you are!"

He was literally roaring at me in that voice that sounded like a concrete mixer with gravel tumbling in the bottom. I managed to force out a labored, "Yes sir, coach!" He pushed me back a bit and let go of the face mask. "Okay, then, let's get back to work," he said as he turned his back to me and started toward the tower. "I better never have to have this talk with you again, son." And he never did. For all the years I played my heart out for him at Alabama, and for many years thereafter, I felt like he coached me individually with a lot more negative than positive reinforcement. Regardless, he was a great coach to play for and he taught me a lot. And with that uncertain endorsement from

Coach Bryant, I left Bama full of ego and vanity, but I somehow endured to become a nationally recognized pro football player with my face staring out of a helmet on the cover of *Sports Illustrated,* the most prestigious sports magazine on the planet.

Some people would say my life was the American Dream come true. Maybe in their eyes they were right. In mine the truth is that most of my life and pro career were more of a living nightmare than a dream because the man I saw in the mirror each day was someone I never really knew. The real me was a little boy in a champion's body trying to make his daddy happy by emulating the pro football players I had watched growing up. I wanted to become one of those players so badly I became an impostor, posing as "John Hannah: The Best Offensive Lineman of All Time." Until I finally outgrew that mission and found myself in Psalm 73—the number I wore for my entire college and professional careers—the drive to become a player like I idolized and to please my father in the process detracted from every other meaningful relationship I had. In striving to be the best in every game or competition, I never completed the development of my personality, nor did I truly get to know my Heavenly Father. Both of these shortcomings drastically affected my quality of life and ultimately frustrated bonding with my own son.

The brutally honest fact is that my trophies and success were not gained from pursuing ideals. They were medals I won fighting against God's will. They were ribbons, plaques, crystal, and brass awards I weighted myself down with as I guarded the true inner me. I was rewarded and decorated for hiding inside a uniform as I pursued a myopic goal of defining my image as the best athlete I could be.

Even though it took a lifetime to realize it, I now know it all began by misunderstanding some basic lessons of life that my dad taught me as a boy. When I displayed some sensitive personality traits of introspection and compassion as a child, I mistakenly thought he strongly deterred those because he encouraged me to show him how tough I was or how well I played football. I began to fear letting him down—or worse—doing something on or off the field that would disappoint him and embarrass me.

My life became about developing a superathlete/football player image. I was dazzled by the big-name players I watched growing up and wanted to be like them. I wanted to become an even better player than they were and to gain fame and recognition for my efforts beyond my wildest dreams. I also wanted to please my dad and earn his continued praise and I thought becoming the best football player I could was the only way to do that. Reaching that goal required controlling everything and everyone else in my life to keep them focused on me and my athletic strengths. It wasn't until I was well into my 50s that I realized the image I chased all those years had actually become an obsession that enslaved me. I guarded everything else about my true character and personality, so that no one—my dad, my peers, and later even my own children—would ever see my perceived weaknesses of sensitivity and compassion, my God-given traits of humanity, which I felt would do nothing but create disappointment.

Now the need to honor your father is not necessarily bad, for that is one of the Ten Commandments. But when that need begins to subordinate your relationship with God and forces you to adopt a false face and an impostor image to please both of them and become obsessed with building that image, the need becomes an issue of unhealthy control, which retards your spiritual growth and stunts the development of relationships with others based on trust and respect. I was born into unique circumstances with a father who was a former professional football player, a brilliant and highly protective mother, and a set of genetics that would quickly elevate me into the company of world-class athletes. But from a very early age, my sensitive personality led to a lifelong struggle between my body and soul. Unfortunately, as my size and athletic skills outgrew my mind and heart at a grossly disproportionate rate, the struggle to maintain a balance between all these human dynamics also began sooner than I was able to understand them much less handle them.

The power of defining my identity as a gifted athlete while suppressing those deeper personality traits was addictive. The larger my athletic image became, the harder I pushed to stifle the inner me. The need to maintain control of enhancing one and subordinating the other became a destructive obsession that took its toll on me and most of my other personal relationships. Just as addictive substances ultimately cause harm and damage to a person and those around them, controlling something in one's life is no less addictive and in some ways potentially more destructive to relationships and commitments.

As with every addiction, nothing good ever comes from them. In my case the more control I exercised in growing my image as a jock and suppressing the sensitive inner me, the more damage I did to my relationships with my friends and family and ultimately with my dad. The larger my adopted and false image became, the more I hurt the ones I wanted to please the most. I'm still making up ground for all those decades I all but ignored my maker, but I am glad to know now that He has never once given up on me. One of my favorite bluegrass song titles is "I'm Not Holding on to Him, He's Holding Onto Me," and that's how I see my relationship with Him now.

Doesn't that sound strange coming from someone who sports pundits otherwise called "the best"? By driving myself harder and harder to be the best, I stiff-armed the real me in the process. Looking back on those days, I am utterly dismayed at how much of my life I misused and wasted living by that warped way of thinking. That muddy road from Alabama to Foxborough was cloaked in darkness and doubt even with the glaring stadium lights and blinding flashbulbs.

I hid inside that football helmet and jersey. I guarded my inner personality with shoulder pads. I denied God's voice calling to me by listening only to the roaring crowds because I wanted them—the fans—to really like me and I guess I always just assumed I didn't have to do much to have God like me. After all He made me the way I was with an extraordinary amount of talent. I mistakenly thought it was okay for me to take what gifts He had given me and run with them as far as I could without realizing I was actually running away from Him by seeking constant glory and fame through those talents instead of always honoring Him first.

Until my stubborn ox was completely ditched, I never truly experienced God's grace and accepted that He made me a man in his image rather than just a great football player. Only after being broken would I finally accept his love and forgiveness for my refusal to accept his omnipotence. As with other addicts, his blessing came to me only after I had recklessly inflicted unbelievable damage to my body and soul and caused unnecessary personal loss to myself and others.

By viciously controlling my prowess on the field and hiding my weaknesses and vanity inside that uniform, I couldn't see I was wrongfully trying to earn his love rather than accepting it completely. Because I was struggling to make him love me so hard, I had to be broken—knocked to my knees, beaten, trounced, and bloodied in my heart—to realize I didn't have to earn his love and become his child. The person I used to be—the tough Hog from Alabama—was nothing more than a bloated personality driven by a massive ego who believed success was attained by *my* efforts alone. But as I was finally compelled to acknowledge God's amazing grace, I acknowledged that "Hog" the football player was just an opaque, fleeting image that I built and which led only to temporary success and self-deception. My eyes slowly opened as I began to shed the impostor I had become. The biggest challenge I ever faced was to break away from the mind-set that had sustained me.

Although the roaring player on the football field was really just a disguise and the impostor inside protected me from emotional harm, the little child wanted him to leave, but he stayed and grew larger and larger as he was decorated with medal after medal and award after award. That impostor enslaved me so that I did what I thought that image required of me, and by keeping Hog the football player front and center, I ended up keeping God somewhere in the distant secondary.

I hated living a lie, but I did not know how else to live my life. The more recognition I got from my image as an athlete and football player, the more submerged my real personality became. I found myself permanently stuck in a role that identified me, instead of vice versa. The chains and armor by which that image held me captive were too adorned and engraved. The food and drink of fame that image brought me were too rich and filling. I was like the man in the iron mask. That impostor face cost me a lot in my relationships with other people, but most especially it kept me away from a true relationship with God for a long, long time. Until God flattened me like never before, broke me from the belief that I was in total control, and stripped me of the heavy armor, I was nothing.

Psalm 73
A Psalm of Asaph
Surely God is good to Israel,

To those who are pure in heart.
But as for me, my feet had almost slipped;
I had nearly lost my foothold
For I envied the arrogant,
When I saw the prosperity of the wicked.
They have no struggles;
Their bodies are healthy and strong.
They are free from the burdens common to man;
They are not plagued by human ills.
Therefore, Pride is their necklace;
They clothe themselves with violence.
From their callous hearts comes iniquity,
The evil conceits of their minds know no limits.
They scoff and speak with malice;
In the arrogance they threaten oppression.
Their mouths lay claim to Heaven,
And their tongues take possession of the earth.
Therefore, their people turn to them and drink
    up waters in abundance.
They say, "How can God know? Does the Most
    High have knowledge?"
This is what the wicked are like—
Always carefree, they increase in wealth.
Surely in vain have I kept my heart pure;
In vain have I washed my hands in innocence.
All day long I have been plagued;
I have been punished every morning.
If I had said, "I will speak thus," I would have
    betrayed your children.
When I tried to understand all this, it was
    oppressive to me
'Til I entered the sanctuary of God;

Then I understood their final destiny.
Surely you have put them on slippery ground;
You cast them down to ruin.
How suddenly are they swept away by terrors!
As a dream when one awakes, so when You rise,
    O Lord,
You will despise them as fantasies.
When my heart was grieved and my spirit
    embittered,
I was senseless and ignorant.
I was a brute beast for you.
For I am always with you;
You hold me by my right hand.
You guide me with your counsel,
And afterward you will take me into your Glory.
Whom have I in Heaven but you?
And earth has nothing I desire but you.
My flesh and heart may fail,
But God is the strength of my heart
And my portion forever.
Those who are far from you will perish;
You destroy all who are unfaithful to you.
But for me, it is good to be near God.
I have made the sovereign Lord my refuge;
I will tell of all your good deeds.

CHAPTER 2

A Southern Family

TO GIVE YOU a concise account of my early history—some would call it ancient history—I was born on April 4th, 1951, in Canton, Georgia, to Herb and "Coupe" Hannah. My mother's real name was Geneva, but when she and Dad started dating, he said she was as pretty and sleek as a '37 Chevy coupe. So he nicknamed her "Coupe," which stayed with her for the rest of her life. They were salt of the earth people who married while they were still in college, even though he was at Alabama and she was at the University of Georgia. They were from what most would call "the country." My parents both had particularly hard childhoods for reasons I'll explain, but they were a loving, hardworking couple, and my earliest memories are full of nothing but love and security.

From the day I was born, I was called "John Allen." Not John, Johnny, J.A. but…John Allen. I was named after my two grandfathers, John Watkins and Allen Hannah. I guess that's one of those Southern things, kind of like Ellie Mae, Betty Sue, or John Paul, a special favorite of rural Southern Baptists in the early 1950s. It wasn't until I was in the sixth grade that I became known simply as John. It was a matter of choice—not by me—but by a teacher, who had two Allen's in her classroom. Not wanting to confuse the names of her students, she asked me if I wanted to be known as either John or Allen. I chose John. I'm glad I did because somehow I just can't see me having the career and recognition I did if I had been *Allen* "Hog" Hannah.

Dad's father-in-law, Grandfather Watkins, was a kind man who worked hard and built a successful dairy in Canton, which bore his name. Grandmother Watkins, however, was a stern woman with a sharp tongue who, I came to learn, was ashamed of my mother and her second daughter, Geneva. She was resentful because Mom had been previously married at a young age and then quickly divorced from a hateful older man, who beat her but fathered my half-brother, Ron. He was a good brother to me, Charley, and David, and Dad adopted him as one of his own. He looked remarkably like my mother, and in the family portrait of us four Hannah boys, you can tell he looked nothing like the rest of us, who were Dad's blood sons. He wasn't athletic, but he was smart as a steel trap and later became the accountant for the Hannah family business. Ron died several years ago from cancer, and I still miss him.

Mom was a beautiful woman, tall and slender with delicate, aquiline features, sandy blond hair, and blue eyes. She also had a very sharp mind and was the head of secretarial sciences at the University of Georgia. Even though she was absolutely brilliant and was later led on a path to become a high-ranking business executive with IBM, she subordinated her career to allow my dad to follow his football career to the professional level. Still Grandmother Watkins remained ashamed of her because she believed her second daughter brought embarrassment to the Watkins family name by marrying too young and having a child with a worthless man. Mom never talked about the difficult relationship with her mother, but I recall sensing as a child that Mom and her mother never got along very well. I never knew why until many years later when Dad told me about Mom's first marriage and how her mother treated her. Although I never had much affection for Grandmother Watkins to begin with, I had even less after knowing how worthless she made Mom feel.

When I was born, we lived in a small house without running water behind the Watkins Dairy and across the creek from my aunt and uncle, who also worked in the dairy. Dad told me that when I was born, he installed a manual water pump in the house, so Mom wouldn't have to draw water from the creek. Although we certainly weren't rich by any means, I wouldn't say we were poor. But I guess when somebody gives their wife a hand pump to put running water in the house, that's scraping the bottom of the money chain.

Dad was big and brawny with olive skin, large muscles, jet black hair, and a massive jaw. When he smiled he absolutely beamed with a nearly perfect set of white teeth. He could be gregarious and playful or stern and confrontational. After bypassing college right out of high school because World War II had started, he spent nearly four years in the war as a navy pilot. When the war was over, he enrolled in the University of Alabama and had a very successful career playing football. In fact he was good enough to be drafted by the New York Giants to play professional football in 1951, the year I was born. He was a man who had little fear and a natural intolerance for weakness and irresponsibility. He was a disciplinarian, too, but he never once made me feel unloved—even when he punished me.

He was a good man and a very good father. His toughness no doubt came from a rough start in life with his own father, "Daddy Hannah." For a number of years, my grandfather was an abusive drunk when Dad was a kid, and Daddy Hannah would disappear for months at a time leaving him, Uncle Gene, and Granny Hannah to fend for themselves. Granny Hannah couldn't read or write, but she was the most loving, forgiving person I think I've ever known. I'm sure she endured a lot more heartache and misery than I know, but Daddy Hannah had a taste for cheap liquor and cheaper women, and when Dad was only eight years old, he disappeared so long that Granny Hannah couldn't take care of Dad and Uncle Gene, so she had no choice but to sell them out as sharecroppers to a farmer in Mississippi. That's right. Dad basically lost his father, his momma, and his childhood when he was eight.

Dad told me later that he remembers when he was a very young boy members of the Ku Klux Klan stormed into his house and dragged Daddy Hannah outside where they tied him to a tree and horse-whipped him within an inch of his life for being a derelict father, who didn't take care of his wife and children.

Dad and Uncle Gene were eventually able to return home after Daddy Hannah came back long enough to sober up, and Granny took him back. As I said, she was so forgiving that I'm sure she understood the alcohol had poisoned her husband, and when he quit drinking, he returned to the man she used to love. It took a long time, however, for Dad and his father to eventually reconcile. But they did, and after my father became successful, he bought Daddy Hannah a house in Albertville, Alabama, where he lived the rest of his life. Still my memories of Daddy Hannah are not pleasant at all. As far as I was concerned, he was just an ornery old man. He always treated me as someone unworthy of talking to, and I never once felt the urge to cry at his funeral. Despite the fact I didn't like Daddy Hannah very much and didn't miss him when he was gone, I have no doubt my father's reconciliation with his father was God's will. It would be an example for me later when it became necessary for me to ask for God's strength in order reconcile with my own children.

Because of his rough upbringing, playing college and professional football and Navy service in WWII, Dad naturally expected me to be tough and stand on my own from an early age. After some very traumatic events in my grammar school years, he taught me to fight for what I thought was right and to never let anyone get the better of me without giving it my best effort. I was also fed well as a child. I needed a lot of food because my genetics demanded it and—besides that—I just loved to eat. A lot. By the time I entered kindergarten, I was already substantially bigger and heavier than most of the other kids. Mom told me that other mothers would ask her at the grocery store, "What are you feeding that boy?" or "Lord, that boy is getting *big!* I bet you're glad you don't have to carry him on your hip anymore."

Just before I started first grade, my youngest brother, David, was born, and Dad had to quit his football coaching job at the local Canton high school. He didn't think he could support a wife and three young boys on a coach's salary. But before he quit, I used to tag along with him to football practice. I remember well the smell of freshly mown grass, the clash of players tackling each other, and being babysat by the cheerleaders who took good care of "the coach's son." Those feel-good memories of time with my dad define my earliest years, and even after those feelings temporarily changed a few years later, I always felt very close to him and the pride he showed in me.

Soon, however, the time came when I didn't love him so much and began to resent his trying to control me. At times I was certain that he hated me because I had disappointed him or that I could never do anything well enough to make him proud. I labored under those misconceptions for years, but they were dispelled in 1991 when he gave the opening speech before my induction into the Pro Football Hall of Fame in Canton, Ohio. As a former professional player himself, he was the first father ever permitted to make such introductory remarks for a son, and that singular event was perhaps the finest moment we ever shared.

Charley was born when I was four. I was not quite seven when David came along. Suddenly, there was competition in the house. Although my half-brother, Ron, had always been in the picture, he was older than I, so I was the baby of the family and had received all the attention. When the new son arrived and then the next, something changed. I was no longer the only prince in the castle. If I wanted to keep the king's attention and pride, I was going to have to work very hard for it.

CHAPTER 3

A Childhood Hurt
Leads to the Gridiron

W HEN I WAS in the fourth grade, I had the first real shock and emotional trauma of my life. I know all kids go through hurtful events and circumstance when they are young that forever change the way they see things. In this day and age, the instant access to news through the 24/7 media coverage probably brings more horrifying events to light than we could have ever imagined back when I was young. Things we see and read about that happen to kids these days are much worse by a mile than what I'm about to describe. What I'll tell you may sound downright absurd in its insignificance in the grand scheme of things, but at the time it happened, it left a very real emotional scar on me.

By the time I was nine, I had grown to be a very large and obese fourth grader. I was also a *huge* mama's boy. I was as innocent and naïve as a child could be and didn't have a clue that people could be really mean and hateful to each other—much less that your seemingly trustworthy friends could turn on you and become tormenters in a flash by teasing you painfully and mercilessly. I didn't really have a sense of self-image back then. The thought of how other people might see me had never entered my mind. Looking back at pictures from those years, I was *really* fat and embarrassingly so. My belly was almost bigger around than I was tall, and my face was so pudgy that my eyes looked like they were squinted shut. I don't ever remember anyone telling me I was fat. I certainly never heard anyone tease me about it or saying hurtful things about me being fat. But that changed very quickly and without warning.

One day during recess, some of my childhood friends, guys I trusted and liked, suddenly turned on me and began calling me "Fatty, Fatty, two by four!" in that kind of sing-song way that kids do. They began running around me, singing that phrase over and over. "Fatty, Fatty, two by four! Can't get through the bathroom door!" I was shocked and felt a strange, jolting hurt like nothing else before. All of a sudden, I was singled out and ridiculed. I was suddenly no longer an accepted member in this circle of friends. In that instant I experienced the utter despair of discovering in one explosive round of collective insults and epithets that I was a failure, an inadequate, undesirable loser, someone who was so different from all the rest that I couldn't possibly belong in the group any more. I immediately felt branded as a pariah, an outcast, a human without worth, a leper everyone should avoid at all cost.

They had blindsided me worse than I ever got hit in my future football career. I couldn't get them to stop, and they just kept going on and on. I had no idea what I had done to deserve this unmerciful taunting, why they started it, or what I could do about it.

When I realized that I was even bigger and fatter than almost every fifth grader and most of the sixth graders, it literally tore me up inside. I remember walking home, sobbing about it, looking for my parents to comfort me. However, their reaction—

especially my father—to the awful pain and hurt I was describing didn't console me at all. Looking at it now with a bit of armchair psychoanalysis, I guess back then a parent—especially a father being able to coddle a young son's sensitivity to his emerging sense of self—might not have been as easy as it ought to have been. We were just barely a few years out of the horrible aftermath of World War II when boys had to become men overnight and then grow into soldiers the day after that. So there was little room for bruised childhood egos or feeling sorry for oneself.

While I was still crying and moping, Dad made a phone call that would change my life.

He called one of his former student-athletes, Jim Cramer, who was coaching the sixth through eighth grade football team, and asked him if I could try out for the team. I don't know what all was said between them but have imagined many times how that conversation must have gone. After a while Dad came to my room, sat down, and talked to me like a man. I remember him saying very clearly, "Son, I think I know a way to get them to stop teasing you. Try out for the football team. If you want them to quit picking on you and laughing about how big you are, getting on the football team will sure do it. A fourth grader playing with the sixth, seventh, and eighth graders will sure make 'em stop teasing you. You've got the size and speed to be a good player if you'll try it and stick with it and if you to try out. I already called the coach, who said he'll let you. What do ya' say, huh?"

I always thought I would play football someday when I got old enough, but the thought of starting to play when I was only in the fourth grade was something that had never crossed my mind, so I asked him, "Do you think I really could?" He looked me in the eyes and said, "I do, son, and I'll be real proud of you if you do. And when you make the team, which I'm sure you will, you give it the best you can, okay?"

Suddenly the whole emotional shock and trauma of being teased about my size and branded a fat loser led to an open door my dad showed me and through which I would walk into another life. Me on a team! Me being good enough at age nine to play with the junior high kids!

He went on in a very encouraging voice I had never quite heard before, a voice tinged with some excitement. "If you quit before you've become the absolute best player you can be, you'll *never* have anyone's respect in anything else you'll ever do, John, *never*. People will always know you as a quitter. And people don't respect quitters," he said. "Sure, it'll be hard work, but give it your best and put everything you have right down there on the line, and there's no telling where it will take you. You're going to keep growing and getting much stronger in the next few years, John, and it'll be a good way to get in shape and knock off some of that flab, okay? I guarantee those kids won't tease you anymore about being big, either."

I sat there feeling both a little better but also a little scared at the prospect of what my dad was encouraging me to do. Still the excitement of me as a fourth grader actually pulling it off and *making* the team was starting to settle in. Trying to hide my uncertainty that I could actually do what he said, I simply replied, "Yes, sir."

■ | | | | ■

I don't remember the exact sequence of how things unfolded as I tried to heal that early schoolyard assault to my ego by weaving football into the remedy, but I took my dad's advice and tried organized football for the first time. And then…it began. My life on the gridiron set up a lifelong quest to become the best football player I could be.

Dad called the coach back and told him I was going to try out for the team. Fall practice had already begun a week or so earlier, so I was getting a late start. I tried on some eighth grade uniforms, and Dad found me a used pair of cleats at a yard sale. He went into town by himself and also bought me an old helmet with a thick plastic face mask. When he brought that thing home to me, I remember he helped me put it on and showed me how to tie the chin strap. After making sure it fit okay, he sat back and smiled that big pearly white grin at me and said, "There you have it—John Allen Hannah, the football player! You look good, son, real good!" I stared back at him out of that old face mask and thought that smile on his face was the most wonderful sight I had ever seen in my life. It was a sight I would spend the next 30 years of my life striving to see every time I put a helmet on.

I also have to confess I was scared to death the day we started practice because all the other guys just seemed so much older and cockier than I could have ever guessed. I remember hiding and vomiting behind a boxwood bush just before I walked up to the playing field and I prayed I wouldn't do that again where anybody could see how nervous and scared I really was. The other players laughed and made fun of me being the "Baby Huey" of the team and basically dismissed me as some sort of dork trying to be something he wasn't. Although I had grown up around football and heard my dad use all the terms and knew what the positions were, I didn't know much of anything about the actual techniques used. I also didn't know how tough and physically demanding football actually was but learned that lesson on the first day I walked onto the practice field. I was determined to listen to everything the coach was saying and try as hard as I could because my dad was watching from the fence.

To my surprise I quickly found out that my exceptional size allowed me as a fourth grader to actually compete with the sixth and seventh graders. Now you have to remember that the difference in size and maturity (both physically and mentally) between someone in the fourth grade as compared to another boy in the seventh or eighth grade is light years different. But because I was so freakishly big at that age, I could actually push the other kids around by using my weight if I really strained. I still got pushed around and beaten up a lot until I realized the intensity I needed to use. To reach that point, I almost had to get really angry. With a little guidance from the coach, I discovered that if I actually used the strength in my legs to push the other guy back, I could drive—not just push—him out of the way.

The coaches yelled encouragement at me, "C'mon, boy! Use those legs! Hit him! Hit him!" And they would send other older, stronger players into the lineup to see if they could match me. It quickly became apparent there were only a few boys who could stand up against me for very long. Some of them began jawing at each other "Dang, boy! You let a fourth grader whip your bee-hind! Your daddy's gonna be mad at you!" or "What you doing letting Baby Huey push you 'round, Jack? That's a fourth grader, man!"

The unbelievable surge of confidence I got from those very first days of trying football was clearly motivating. Suddenly I stood out for something other than being big and fat. I was the big and chunky football player, and people began to notice me as someone they could be proud of, especially my dad. I remember after the first practice or two, the coach called my dad all excited and said, "Herb, that boy is a natural! You saw how he's pushing all those other kids around even most of the eighth graders! There's not a one of 'em that can stand up to him! That's the most amazing thing I've seen in all my year's coaching! And as young as he is, he's going to get a *whole* lot better and quickly!"

Dad reinforced the high I was on by saying to me (possibly for the first time) "Son, I'm proud of you, boy. Keep it up, and there's no telling how far you'll go. See, I told you that if you tried football and continue to give it your best, other people will respect you more and quit teasing you about being fat. They'll pay more attention to you, too, and won't call you names anymore." And after that Dad came to my practices and watched me from over the fence. Afterward he would always tell me the same thing over and over again. It made me feel really good that I was making him proud instead of letting him down.

I started the first game of the season that year I was in the fourth grade. Back then we played both ways, meaning the starting players lined up on both offense and defense. Making this team and actually starting with the eighth graders gave me a feeling of acceptance and accomplishment like I could never describe. As the game got started, and the hits started coming, they were different from the hits we had taken in fall practice scrimmages. They were *real* hits and they were delivered with an intense motive to beat us. The other team was our enemy, and every player across the line was somebody I wanted to beat, somebody I *had* to beat. In that first actual conflict on the field, I felt something come alive inside me, a surge of energy and entitlement I couldn't describe, but it was a power, a force, whatever you call it, that I knew was mine and I liked it.

Around the start of the second half, my teammates had accepted me and were shouting out, "Hold him, Hannah!" "Hit him! Hit him!" "Keep him off me, Hannah!" "Git him, John, run him down!" "Good job, dude!" The fact I was contributing some good plays and actually being encouraged and counted on by my teammates pumped my confidence and commitment up to the sky. Then in one particularly hard play where the tackles caused several of us to crash to the ground in a big heap, I smashed my nose against the front of that old helmet Dad had bought me and busted my nose. It started bleeding like crazy. Blood ran down my chin and onto my jersey, and when the coach saw me bleeding, he called me out of the game as soon as the play was over. He made me take off my helmet and got in close to my face for a look. "I think it may be broken, John. I need you to come on out of the game, so we can get it looked at."

I immediately answered, "But I don't care, Coach, I wanna play. It'll be okay when I get home." I wasn't whining or pleading. I just really wanted to keep playing.

"I don't know, John. That looks pretty bad, and I *really* think you ought to come on out," Coach said. The look of disappointment on my face, even covered in sweat and blood, must have been unmistakable, and then he hesitated and said, "Let me go talk to your dad a minute." He came back and said, "Your dad wants to talk to you, John."

I hustled over to the fence where Dad was waiting for me, and as soon as he got a look at my nose, he said, "It's broken, John. You need to come on out of the game, and we'll put ice on it before you make it any worse."

"But Dad, I really want to keep playing," I said. "Please? Please? I *really* want to stay in the game, please? It'll be alright. Please?"

God bless him, my dad recognized the fire in my eyes, and his own eyes softened as he said, "Okay, buddy, okay. Tell coach I said it's okay, and we'll take care of it later. As I grinned and started to turn on my heel, he said, "Hey, John Allen…I'm proud of you, son. You're doing real good."

After that and over the next few years, I couldn't wait for another game to roll around. Playing football began to consume most of my thoughts. I took an intense interest in learning as much as I could about different teams and players and what techniques and strategies worked in any given play during a game. As notice and praise about my skills from others started rushing in, quite frankly, I became obsessed with football. With that obsession also came the need for more and more recognition as John Allen Hannah, the football player. That moniker started defining who I was to become. Now I was more than just John Allen Hannah, the fat little farm kid. I began to realize that I could make my father and other people pay attention to me instead of making fun of me. I noticed my father was clearly paying closer attention to me and perking up when other dads would tell him how good I was or how I could play in the big leagues if I stayed with it and worked hard.

I also learned how to play Little League baseball around that time and quickly became a pretty mean catcher. I learned how to throw my shoulder into a runner at home and liked hitting them pretty hard to stop a run. I also started running track and learned the right way to toss a shot put, hurl a discus, and throw a javelin. My father was also very proud of me for taking up these sports, too, but it became clear he mainly reinforced his love and pride for me more in football terms. Regardless of what sport I was competing in, I came to believe athletics was the only way I could earn love and pride from him. Even though Momma stayed on me about my schooling and praised good grades, it was not with the same enthusiasm or excitement that Dad showed when I played well. He and I began to share a bond that very soon would revolve almost exclusively around my performance in athletics and specifically my excelling as a football player.

In years since I have also often wondered whether my dad—by focusing our relationship so exclusively on football—was somehow living vicariously through me to recapture his old playing days. Later when I played with the Patriots, I really began to wonder if my success was making up for an inner insecurity of his about not being good enough to play in the pros since he quit after only one season with the Giants. That was a question I never voiced with him, and one he never voluntarily answered as long as he lived.

■ | | | | ■

I took a lot more interest in watching the pro football games on Sunday afternoon after church, chores, and homework were finished. I began to imagine what it would be like to be one of those players, and how it would feel if my name became recognized by thousands of fans. I began wondering what kind of life those guys had off the field and imagined they had sports cars, nice homes, and anything else they wanted. What I also knew was that they had respect from others, and they were the cool guys who were like the superhuman heroes of our country. Young guys my age didn't look up to soldiers and business executives and point to them and say, "When I grow up, I want to be just like that guy." No, football and baseball players were the role models that most of my generation idolized. They are who we wanted to emulate. They had the image—that so many kids like me wanted to achieve—of toughness, fame, and fortune. It didn't matter that many of them were downright arrogant and condescending. They were entitled to be that way because they could. That's the image I began to focus on exclusively, and I wanted to be among those players whose name everyone would recognize as being the best of the best.

Many decades later, as I got bigger, stronger, and better, I realized the goal of attaining that image became an infatuation. Then it became a mission. The closer I got, reaching the pinnacle of pro football was my Holy Grail. It became my obsession, something I was ultimately addicted to. But when it all collapsed and fell apart, I came to understand that I had indeed been living my life just as Asaph had written in Psalm 73:

> I envied the arrogant when I saw the prosperity of
>   the wicked;
> They have no struggles, their bodies are healthy
>   and strong.
> They are free from the burdens common to man;
>   they are not plagued by human ills;
> Therefore, pride is their necklace, and they clothe
>   themselves with violence.

By being the best player on the line and someone who would not back down from a fight off the field, I knew my dad and everybody else would respect me. As I grew older, the principles of full contact football simply became my way of handling life. Not only was I going to put every ounce of my being on the line to prove I was better than anyone else, I was also going to stay on the offense in every relationship and control them at all cost, no matter how arrogant or condescending I might appear to others. Only now do I fully realize how offensive my conduct was.

Maintaining control of that image in every situation, so that no one would ever get the better of me, is what propelled me through life with the myopic focus of a thundering bull. I also had to maintain control because I couldn't fully trust anybody for fear they would turn on me in a second. That mind-set drove me as a younger man through the football teams of Baylor High, the Albertville High School, the University of Alabama, and the New England Patriots. It also followed me home and tore into the intimate relationships with my family, my brothers, my first wife and kids, Seth and Mary Beth. My arrogance in maintaining superiority also tainted nearly every friendship and business deal I became involved with.

CHAPTER 4

The Rough and Tumble Hannah Boys

THROUGH THOSE NEXT few years after fourth grade, I began to assume the appearance of a football player. I also adopted some of the affectations of other players I'd seen with stern and glaring game faces. I consciously made myself frown and stare with a clenched jaw when I got off a school bus or ran onto a field. I began walking around with my fists balled up like I was going to hit the first person who got in my way. Although I was born with a left foot that turns in and makes me walk like a duck, I consciously developed a swagger in my gait not unlike a gorilla rocking side to side and I began to yell every time I hit someone on the field.

I thought to myself that by looking meaner than I was, opposing players would think, *Did you see the look on that guy's face? He looks like he's ready to tear someone's head off.* Frankly, I liked being someone else and hiding behind that face mask. It felt secure and empowering. I grew an attitude that the better I got, the more comfortable I was becoming as this person who was different from my real self.

That devastating mind-set followed me into my adult years. It made me feel that if I ever quit intimidating or impressing people, others wouldn't be proud of me or love me as much. Ferocity and competitiveness were the only tools I learned to use to earn people's respect. Everything else became secondary and mostly irrelevant.

The early seeds of that attitude also brewed and grew into my relationships with my younger brothers, Charley and David. We loved either other, but we played very hard with each other. Well, "play" might not be the right word—more like fighting. We fought all the time and when we would tangle up, it was often bloody and painful, and someone would get hurt. Charley, who was four years younger than I and always smaller and faster, knew how to push my buttons precisely and he became very persistent at it. As he would say later in life, "My best tool against John was to hit him and then run as fast as I could and go hide somewhere where he couldn't get to me until he had cooled off." David was the youngest and usually tried to make peace between all of us, but when he got older and bigger, he'd get right in the middle and make it a three-way fight, and you never knew who was helping who.

How did Charley hide from me for all those years? It would drive me absolutely crazy, and he would rub it in, even though I would threaten to beat the living snot out of him if he didn't tell me where he hid. I never figured it out until he told me his secret many moons later. He said he would intentionally lie in wait for me somewhere in our house and then hit me or throw something at me and then take off and disappear. Even though I would tear the house apart trying to find him or storm the yard and bushes trying to catch him, he would hide from me until I cooled off, which sometimes took a couple hours, and then he'd reappear—almost as if by magic. When I asked him later when we were in our 20s and all at home for one particular Christmas how he could do that and where did he go, he said, "Do you remember that long hallway between all the bedrooms, the door to the basement, and mom and dad's room? Whenever I'd tag you, I'd take off down that hallway, run by the basement door and slam it real hard on my way by, so you'd think I had jumped down the steps and gotten outside before you could reach me. But I'd keep on running right into mom and dad's room, shut the door real quiet, and then slip into their bathroom. Do you remember that big towel cabinet up over the vanity? I could stand on the sink, climb up in that cabinet, and curl up in a real tight ball while I waited for you to calm down or give up looking for me. One time I had to stay up there almost two hours. You were so mad at me, and I cramped up so bad I almost couldn't get out."

When Charley finally told me that, I hit him so hard in the midsection that I knocked the wind out him. "That's payback I still owe you, brother," I said. He took it in good humor, I'm glad to say.

One particular Christmas, we all got BB guns, and the war was on. When Mom and Dad weren't looking, we used to have a game to see who was the toughest. It was a game of chicken, which I bet, not many other brothers have ever played. We'd stand maybe 30 feet apart, and one of us would turn around, and the other one would shoot you in the back. Charley would shoot David, David would shoot me, and then I'd shoot Charley. Everything except the back of the head was fair game: shoulders, buttocks, legs, back, everything. Then we'd take another step closer to each other, and do it all over again. We did that until one would finally quit. The two left standing would shoot it out until the other brother quit, and there would be a winner. The "toughest Hannah alive," we'd call it.

One time when I was maybe 15 and Charley was 11, we were working at my dad's store helping unload 100-pound bags of feed. I was already strong enough that I could heave a bag up onto a pallet where Charley would catch them and line them up in a row. It was hard work. I mean *really* hard work. After a few hours, I was barking at Charley, bullying him around, and claiming that I figured I had thrown maybe two tons of feed up there while he had just moved them around in straight lines. Charley got really mad, and when I wasn't looking, he blindsided me with a piece of lead pipe, hitting me in the back as hard as he could. He took off running across the parking lot toward the warehouse. I started after him. His plan was to jump up maybe six feet into the warehouse and hide between the forklifts and pallets where he knew I couldn't get to him. But just as he made his jump, I caught him by the leg of his blue jeans and pulled him all the way back to the ground where he landed with a huge thud.

I jumped on him and started beating the stew out of him. The next thing I know, I'm choking him with all my might. Suddenly, Dad is right there hollering at me to get off him because I was trying to kill him. David was standing to the side, crying and pleading with me to get off him before I killed him, and Dad had to physically wrestle me off Charley. He hollered at me, "What are you doing, John? You could have killed him!"

When I stood up, I hollered right back, "Well, he deserved to die!"

Another time a little later after that, we were all having family supper, and Mom complained about a cabinet door in the kitchen needing to be tightened. She asked me to go in the basement and get a screwdriver, and as my mom was always into gadgets, I found this little tool I had never seen that looked like it had a flashlight on the end of it. When I came back upstairs looking at it, I asked her what this thing was. Charley didn't miss a beat and said, "That's a light, you big dummy, so you can see what you're about to screw." Quick as a flash, my dad reached across the table and hit Charley square in the chest with his fist as hard as he could. That particularly swift punishment for making an off-color comment in front of Mom left a lasting impression on Charley in more ways than one, especially since Dad was wearing a big gold ring with a heavy stone in the middle, which put a perfectly round red welt and then a bruise just over his heart.

When we first moved to Albertville, Alabama, from Canton, Georgia, I had never really heard any curse words. But, as soon as we got there, I learned a whole bunch of them; I mean nasty, ugly words. I fell in with a crowd of football players and quickly began to use those words a lot when I wasn't around Mom and Dad. I used to call Charley and David everything in the book and then dared them to tell our folks. One afternoon at home, however, I was in a particularly bad mood over something, and Mom jumped on me about something else I'd forgotten to do. Without thinking, I hurled a really offensive curse word at her, calling her the b-word. My dad bolted from his chair and hit me so hard that it knocked me clear across the room. I never used that word in front of my mother ever again.

■ | | | | ■

All three of us boys—me, Charley, and David—grew up working the summers and weekends, helping Dad run the business. Frankly, I guess we also gained some local respect from the established farmers and chicken producers for being the hard working Hannah men and being pretty darn good football players, too. The fact that we boys got that kind of attention from older men, who we also respected and looked up to, added to the pride we took in helping Dad every way we could. That respect also continued to solidify my resolve to be a standout football player as I grew into my early teens.

As Charley and David were growing up, they quickly found themselves living in my shadow, and the sibling rivalry became very intense early in our lives. As I was the biggest and oldest, the notice I got for being a serious football player and all-around athlete drew greater jealousy from my brothers, particularly Charley, even though they earned every right to be noticed on their own merit as exceptional athletes, too. (Charley and David would both earn All-Conference honors at Alabama, and Charley played for the Tampa Bay Buccaneers from 1977 to 1982 and the Los Angeles Raiders from 1983 to 1988.) I suppose that's a big reason we had so many of those fights I told you about. Although Dad had to break up some of the more serious fights between us, he always expected us to stand our ground and not back down from a challenge or a dare. Many times he told us how proud of us he was. We were the Hannahs and had a right to be proud of the family name. He always reminded us: "To be proud of who we were and never do anything to dishonor the family name!"

As the oldest brother, I especially took that to heart. He would often look to me to: "Stand up straight! Show those brothers of yours what a real Hannah is supposed to act like!" It was as if he was using me to set an example for my younger brothers of what a person—a Hannah man—was supposed to act like and be like. I sure didn't want to let him down. When I did let him down, he'd let me know it. He'd give me an earful about my responsibilities and put me in my place as someone who knew better and was supposed to hold the line and "Pave the way for my brothers" to make sure they stood up for the family name.

Sometimes I'd get really steamed at him. Since I was the oldest, I felt like he was being the toughest on me. I thought that was particularly unfair because I had to grow up in much more difficult circumstances than Charley or David did. He should go easier on me than my younger brothers because I had it so much tougher than they did growing up and he should be harder on them because they didn't learn all the hard lessons I had to.

But Hannah boys were a pretty tight team, and as Charley and David began to gain acclaim as excellent athletes and pretty decent guys, I was always very proud of everything they accomplished (even if I didn't tell them that openly). I always believed I had their support and respect, and there was never a question that I loved my brothers immensely and without qualification. Even though our half-brother, Ron, was not Dad's biological child—Dad adopted him when he and Mom married—we never knew any difference in our feelings or relationship with Ron, who died from cancer a few years ago. The only big difference was that Ron was not an athlete of any note. But he never let that bother him. He went to all our games and meets and was always cheering us on with Mom and Dad. Ron was the brains of the family. He graduated from Alabama with a business degree and a 4.0 GPA. He sat for the CPA exam and passed all six sections the first try and eventually became the business and finance manager of Hannah Supply.

Another thing that bound us together was faith in God. Although my folks were people of belief and accepted the holy bible as correct in every sense, we were never fanatical. Bible thumping was not a central part of my youth as it was for so many families in the "Bible Belt" of the South. I had my first religious awakening at the age of nine when I was baptized and pronounced "saved." It was very, very meaningful to me. I took it as acceptance, forgiveness, and responsibility all wrapped up in one big, wet baptismal robe, and it was a big deal for me then. When I heard for the first time that Jesus really loved me so much that He was willing to suffer and die for me on the cross, I took it to heart when I began to understand that his love was something I could always rely on. That faith has endured all my life and stands in stark contrast to the loss of trust in other people I otherwise experienced very early in life.

Although I never lost sight of the fact there was a God who loved me and who gave his son, Jesus, to save us from our mortal sins, I think the virginal buzz of faith started wearing off shortly after my baptism. Life went on, and like a lot of other Christians, I got saved, and that was about the extent of it. No other lightning bolts hit me, no epiphanies or miracles happened, and I just settled back into growing up as a kid with some talent and interest in sports.

My attention turned to football and other sports. At the same time I was budding as a football player, there was schoolwork to do, and a serious conflict began to develop between trying to be a good student and the desire to become a great football player. In my mind I had to make a choice between the two. Education was certainly important, and I maintained good grades, but I prioritized trying to become the absolutely best football player I could, and nothing else was going to stand in the way.

As I continued to grow through my early years, I certainly received correct instructions on both sides of the growth equation in terms of trying to balance a good education against the desire to become a sports star. But during the process, I subordinated many facets of my development to the goal of defining my existence through a football helmet and uniform. The bigger and better I got, the more I crawled inside that image and hid the rest of what humanity and God had blessed me with at birth. The more acclaim I got in sports, the harder it was to express and reconcile the inner me with the outer image I had adopted.

■ | | | | ■

On one other occasion, Charley became so enraged at me, he actually threw a steak knife at me as hard as he could and missed me by just a few inches. It stuck perfectly in one of the kitchen cabinet doors. He was so mad, I think, he really didn't care if he stuck me with it or not. And while we brothers were pretty brutal to each other with often painful results, that particular explosion of temper woke us up a bit to the realization of what might have happened had he actually stabbed me, or worse, killed me. Despite our crazy antics, we brothers loved each other, and David, as the youngest, would often act as peacekeeper or moderator to try and talk some sense into me and Charley to keep us from killing each other or tearing up the house.

Those were rough and tumble years in the Hannah home. The funny thing is—though we fought and played so rough with each other, and it was okay to hit one another—nobody else had that right. For example one of our neighbors had three boys about our age, and they played rough, too. If one of us happened to be over there playing with them, and things got serious to the point where those brothers ganged up on one or two of us, we'd all jump in and fight them together. And if word ever got around that two of us Hannah boys were fighting and anyone jumped in to try and break it up, it'd be the last time they did that because we'd automatically turn on that guy and beat the stew out of him for messing with us.

A lot of things got broken in our house in those early years, and for a long time after we were grown, a wrestling match almost always broke out between us in the first few minutes we got together. We would go at it until everyone had spent themselves completely. After it was over, we'd get up, dust ourselves off, and give each other a man hug. It was like our own way of shaking hands, I suppose.

After those years growing up with my brothers, my ability to intimidate or bully other people into being afraid of me seemed to be my only reliable set of go-to tools I would use in order to take control of a situation. Although it worked in our family, I know how I ruined so many relationships acting that way with other people, but I had adopted that mind-set all those years earlier, and it was really the only one I knew would work and work well.

CHAPTER 5

Not Fighting Back

AFTER DAD REALIZED he couldn't provide for his growing family on a coach's salary, he took a job with the Bradshaw Company, selling farming equipment and poultry supplies. His initial territory was Alabama, which he worked like mad as he commuted to and from Georgia on a weekly basis. What really got to me was—that just as my football persona was emerging—he was away from home a lot. He wasn't around nearly as much as he had been when I first started playing, and it really hurt because I missed him coming to my practices and games. The constant traveling finally got to him.

He quit working for Bradshaw, and we moved to Albertville, Alabama, at the end of my fifth grade year. He and two other guys had started a company called Dixie Poultry Supply, a distributor of animal health products. It sold equipment, supplies, and feed to chicken integrators. It also built and serviced everything from hog pens to chicken wire to aluminum siding, feed grass, medicine, and lighting for commercial hen houses. Dad soon found out he was doing most of the hard work and making most of the sales while the other partners were cashing in on his efforts. When he finally broached the issue, they teamed up against him and tried to push him out. They shouldn't have done that because Dad stood his ground, got the best of them, and forced them to split the company up, and Dad kept the lucrative Alabama territory.

Dad was concentrating on growing his Alabama territory with Dixie Poultry and doing so pretty quickly. His partners over in Georgia, however, began selling in Alabama, which went against their agreement, so Dad simply changed the name of his business to Hannah Supply and began doing business in Georgia. He was very successful, and eventually those guys, who had breached his trust and agreement with him, went out of business, and Dixie Poultry Supply ceased to exist. I had a new insight into my father's personality and began to watch and emulate him as best I could. He was a no-nonsense businessman and gained the farmers' trust and respect as he helped them grow their own businesses, farms, and chicken houses. Dad made a name for himself as a man of his word. He, however, was no pushover. Although he had a soft place in his heart when a particular farmer he knew might fall on a hard patch in the road and Dad would cut him some slack in paying his accounts in full at the agreed due date, God help someone if they ever turned on him.

Folks don't forget someone helping them out when times get tough, and neither did my dad's customers. His business reputation became so well known in the poultry industry that Hannah Supply developed into a major commercial business in the Southeast. Dad worked hard and made quite a success of himself. In the process he also earned some very respectable money and was thereafter able to provide a substantially better way of life for his family and future.

When I look back on it now, I also can see clearly what a starkly different childhood I had compared to Charley's and David's, who were just several years younger than I. They never had to move around. They never had to wonder where Dad was or when he was coming back like I did all those lonely, scary nights as a kid between six and 11 years old. The comparative differences in our earliest years also let me see where our distinctly different personalities and attitudes might have come from.

■ | | | | ■

About the time I was entering the sixth grade at Albertville Elementary, I learned one of the hardest lessons of my life about how to respond to someone trying to push me around. This one event probably started me on the road to using my football mind-set in everyday life and losing the distinction between pushing players around on the field and dealing with adversity in the real world.

It happened on a late summer day with a guy about my age. He wanted to fight me at the ballfield for no reason. He lived up the street from us, and I had no reason to mistrust him or be scared of him. I hadn't done anything to make him mad and—while I hardly even knew him—I thought he was an okay kid. I had no idea why he wanted to fight, and frankly, the very notion of fighting anybody had never entered my mind. In fact the concept of fighting at all was totally foreign to me. Although I was playing football and knocking the stuffing out of opposing players, I never really considered that fighting. It was just a game where we played rough.

But out of the blue, this guy got serious about wanting to fight with me and started jawing at me, poking me in the chest. Then he smacked me pretty hard and started calling me names in that same sing-song voice that the guys did in the fourth grade. He started shoving me and saying stuff like "C'mon, big boy! C'mon! You want some of this?" He began pushing me pretty hard, and I started to stumble backward. When I pushed him back to keep my balance and try to get him to stop, he got mad because I wouldn't fight back. But he didn't stop and only got madder when I pushed him back again. He began pushing and jamming me further, which caused me to rock back on my heels and almost fall. Then he started slugging me in the stomach with balled up fists and hit my arms and ribs as hard as he could. He kept slamming at me and then tried to get me in a headlock. I was throwing my arms up and hollering, "Quit it! What are you doing?" He continued with his assault, though, trying to throw me to the ground or trip me over his ankle with all the strength he could muster. It became apparent he was not about to stop, and by now he was seriously mad.

In a matter of just a few seconds, panic set in, and I just gave up trying to resist. I certainly never fought back. I felt totally defeated and powerless as I was being controlled by this guy who was nowhere as big as I was. In those few awful moments, I realized that I didn't know how to fight. I fell to my knees and covered my face with my arms as I tried to roll over, thinking that if I played possum he would stop. But he didn't. As I lay there, he continued with this public embarrassment on the playground for another few seconds, kicking me as many as 14 or 15 times, many of which hit my big posterior. Billy had literally kicked my butt.

I lay on my stomach on the ground until he gave me a last swift kick in the thigh and then stomped off laughing at me. "Some tough football guy you are, huh?" he said. "You ain't nothing but a big wussy!" I lay there a few more moments until I was certain he had stopped and slowly began to sit up. Everything about me hurt. I was covered in dirt, snot was running out of my nose, and my face was already beginning to swell. I dragged my forearm across my nose and saw a long red streak of blood cross my arm. My eyes were full of tears, though I wasn't actually crying. As I wiped the corners of my eyes, I saw for the first time a couple of other kids who had seen and heard the whole thing. I got up on my knees, staggered as I tried to stand, taking a couple of lurching steps in an effort to regain my balance. And then I saw my dad. He had seen the whole thing.

The kid who beat me up was just one of the neighbors down the street and not really a bad guy. The kid knew I was bigger than he was, but he also knew how naïve I was. I'm not exactly sure why he picked that fight with me, but he was probably just showing off to his buddies that he could whip the big kid.

My mind was reeling as I tried to process what had just happened. My heart was pounding like a jackhammer, and I could barely breathe. The loss of breath I realized was not so much from the physical struggle but rather was from the massive rush of adrenaline, anger, and humiliation that were crashing into each other. I also had a thought flash through my mind that I would never trust this kid again. And for that matter, I wasn't going to trust anybody completely any more. All of a sudden, the memories of those other boys taunting me in fourth grade came rushing back in, and I realized in that same instant I had never trusted those guys ever again either. I dusted myself off as best I could and began the long walk toward my father.

Dad kind of shook his head and said, "You okay, John?" He seemed upset, and I know now he was actually mad at the boy and even madder at himself for not teaching me how to defend myself. But I didn't know that then. I think the fact I didn't fight back really bothered my father more than anything. As I stood there in shock at what had just happened, Dad used a loud and angry voice he'd never directed at me before, "Son, what the heck is wrong with you, boy? Don't you ever let anybody push you around the way that kid did!" Dad said. "I don't ever want to hear about you getting whipped by somebody else unless you have done whatever you had to—picked up a stick or a rock, whatever—or done whatever else you had to do to give him your best shot! You got to stand up for you, boy! You hear me? You're twice as big as that kid, John, and you should have fought back, done something to hurt him because even if he had won with you fighting back, he wouldn't want to do it again because he got hurt doing it. You needed to make him scared of you!"

Those words still sting me like a wasp almost 50 years later. All I could sense right then was that there must be something wrong with me. I felt like a total sissy, a great big failure. But the way I took those words from my father was that because I had not fought back, I had terribly disappointed him, and he did not love me anymore. At that moment the roots of what would become a lifelong addiction sank in. The double whammy of getting my butt beat for the first time and then being harshly chewed out by my father—both of which were intense and painful—welded those events into a conflicting mass of feelings that would fuel my psyche for decades.

I know that sounds overly dramatic, but I bet you can identify with a moment in time when something similar happened that led to a stinging, confusing exchange with your dad. As I stood there with my swollen face and hurt pride, I felt very negative vibes from my father that didn't translate as pride anymore. I couldn't begin to describe whatever it was I was feeling, but my dad's words jolted some things in me that deepened a mind-set that I was never going to let anybody get the better of me again—on or off the football field.

CHAPTER 6

Military School

URING MY EIGHTH grade year, Dad sat me down and told me I was going to attend a private military high school in Chattanooga, Tennessee. The Baylor School was a male-only military academy, and I was being sent there for ninth grade and would actually have to move out of our house. My instant reaction was a fear of losing the comfort and familiarity of my parents, brothers, and friends by moving to another city and living with a bunch of other boys I had never met. When it became apparent that Dad was serious, I had further concerns that it was a military school and I would have to wear a different kind of uniform besides a football jersey and helmet and follow additional military orders beyond the coach's playbooks I was getting familiar with.

Having never been away from home more than a couple of times, I was shocked by the idea. It scared me, and I became strangely uncomfortable as I tried to figure out why Mom and Dad would want to get rid of me, turn me over to someone else to raise, and send me out of their home. I still get a sick feeling to this day when I recall how horrible I felt after they gave me that news.

Why did they send me to Baylor? Dad told me that when he went into the Navy, his formal education and schooling hadn't prepared him well enough to do the math calculations and other tasks necessary to take the Navy pilot's test. Two other cadets befriended him and showed him how to use a slide rule and taught him a few other things they had apparently mastered at Baylor School. He was obviously very grateful that they had helped him, but Dad was the only one of the three who made it through the whole program. Although the Baylor cadets passed the academic tests, they didn't get by some of the physical requirements, and I think Dad always felt bad that those Baylor guys who helped him through didn't make it with him. Regardless, because of their critical help, Dad made a promise to himself back then that if he ever had a son and he could afford it, he was going to send him to Baylor.

After Dad told me that, it changed my attitude somewhat, and I decided if going off to military school made my mom and dad happy and helped Dad repay an old promise he made all those years ago, then I was going to accept it as best I could.

So in the fall of 1965, I entered Baylor. I had just turned 14 earlier that spring, but I was a pretty big kid by then and was proud of the collection of sports trophies I had accumulated in Albertville, Alabama. I spent the summer reading all the required summer books and dreading the day I would leave. When it finally came, I hugged Ron, Charley, and David and got in the car. Mom and Dad spoke very little as we drove up there with my footlocker and other minimal essentials. I didn't know it then, but Baylor's coaching staff was already sizing up the new cadets coming into the ninth grade. A few of the boys they already knew about. I don't think they knew anything about me, but I hoped I might be good enough to at least get a look.

■ | | | | ■

Baylor sits on a beautiful rise on the east bank of the Tennessee River nestled between Lookout and Signal Mountains. It was established in 1893 by a group of Chattanooga businessmen, many of them veterans of the Civil War, who shared a common vision to establish a college preparatory school for the "young men of the city." They sought out Dr. John Roy Baylor, a graduate of the University of Virginia and a supremely distinguished educator, to help establish the school. The philosophy of the school was grounded in its mission to: "Foster in its students both the ability and desire to make a positive difference in the world." Baylor also stressed the military ideals of molding young men into leaders with an appreciation of the South's rich heritage of pride in God, country, and self. Dr. Baylor's vision was to create an institution of secondary education where the innate principles of character and military discipline would be instilled in young sons of the South, so that they would mature into men and leaders with courage and resolve. It was an honorable institution from which hundreds of future business and military leaders graduated, and competition in the field of sports was integral to the military discipline of toughening and sharpening all young men who enrolled there.

The school actively recruited only the most promising or proven coaches and assistants, and in 1965 to be known as a coach of one of the sports teams at Baylor was equivalent to being acknowledged as the best. Baylor's past football teams were legendary, and the excellence of all its other sports teams was nationally known as well. Baylor was also a Mecca for aspiring teachers, and the school enjoyed a well-earned reputation for academic excellence with its faculty members—even the ones who were primarily hired as a coach or assistant. Thus Baylor was highly regarded as an all-around, fine military institution, and parents from all across the country enrolled their sons there in hopes of bettering their stake in life.

I remember my heart rate and anxiety levels rose sharply as I sat in the back of my parents' car, and we approached Baylor's campus. We drove through the imposing brick and stone gates engraved with the school's name and date of establishment and continued over an oak-draped lane past the open football field. We slowly climbed the rising hill toward the buildings and turned into the Quadrangle, which was the school's hub where the American flag proudly presided. The "Quad" was near a stately chapel, the dining hall, Hunter Hall dormitory, and a smaller dormitory at the opposite end of the flagpole called Trustee Hall.

There were numbers of other students and parents arriving, so we were quickly shown our way to the admissions office where all the final formalities of registering and dropping off a boarding student were completed. One of those formalities was being fitted for a military uniform. I was in trouble right away because the school had just switched from seasonal uniforms made of different cloth and gone to a year-round blend of wool. They simply didn't have any year-round wool pants that would fit me. They also didn't have any of the former cotton britches that would fit me either, so I was issued a standard pair of the *heavy* wool pants formerly used in the coldest months. When the training in military drills and marching in formation would begin in a couple of days, I would learn just how hot Chattanooga, Tennessee, could get in the fall.

My dad helped carry my foot locker and a few other things across the Quad, and my folks walked with me to my room in Trustee Hall, the small dormitory that sat between the chapel and dining hall. Back then Trustee Hall only had 10 rooms—five on the first floor and five upstairs. There were also classrooms in the basement where math was taught. I hated math.

As I made up my bed, Dad showed me how to fold precise "hospital corners" at the end of the mattress to keep the sheets taut and crisp for those dreaded military bed inspections. Trying very hard not to cry, they both hugged me tightly, said some parting, tearful words about doing my best and making them proud, and then...they just drove away.

Almost instantly I felt as lost and abandoned as I could ever imagine. I fought back tears of my own and swallowed very hard. The thoughts kept coming to mind that my folks were somehow ashamed of me and had just abandoned me. What was so terribly wrong with me that they would want to get rid of me and foist me off on a jail-like school where I knew no one and had no friends whatsoever?

I was totally and utterly alone. I tried not to get angry, but I failed miserably in keeping those feelings from taking over my complete mind-set. However, being the "tough guy" I was becoming, I buried all those thoughts as best I could and simply stiffened up for the task at hand of surviving the next four years in what I came to feel was a prison.

■ | | | | ■

In the first day or two, the regimented life of a boarding student in a military prep school hit me like a ton of bricks. Everything was precisely structured, and military rules of conduct applied to everything we did—from going to sleep, to waking up, to how we dressed, walked, and addressed other students and teachers. I met many of the other boys on my floor, but some of the upperclassmen—and all of the seniors—would not dare speak to a new boy. That simply wasn't done until the first opportunity of hazing presented itself out from underneath the watchful eyes of a dorm master, a male teacher who lived in the dorm and acted as a surrogate parent. Quickly, I began the immersion with the other new guys into the rumors and inside info about how things really were done at Baylor. The younger brothers of older former Baylor cadets mainly delivered the lessons, and they found some respect by being able to repeat secrets.

One particular memory I have is of this older upperclassman, who used to work in the commissary and hazed me by adopting me as his personal campus transportation service. When he learned I was this really big freshman, he made me bend over and he hopped up on my back like a jockey and made me carry him across the Quad and down the steps to the commissary. After that I had to be there waiting for him when he got through and then he would hop on, and I would carry him back across the Quad and drop him off at his dorm. When he realized I was fast, too, he then started making me run with him on his back, and then I'd run him back after work and so forth. I always wondered about that guy.

The first morning I heard reveille blow at 6:00 AM, I got a real dose of what "regimented" really means. We had to hop out of bed, get dressed in everything except our tie, and be standing at attention outside our doors for a head count five minutes later. Immediately afterward we had to make our beds, straighten everything up, and be spit-shined clean in 20 minutes. A short march to the dining hall for breakfast was followed by four classes a day and then drills—a *lot* of military drills.

Athletics took up the rest of the day, and my schedule was so full that I didn't have much time to mope over my situation. But there were some times early on when I would slip away and climb down one of the sheer hills at the edge of the campus just behind Lupton Hall overlooking the Tennessee River. I would sit on a rock with my arms clenched around my knees and cry my eyes out. I was very careful not to let a soul know where I had gone or what I was doing. I didn't want to get caught showing any emotion, much less be seen crying from homesickness, for fear others would see me as weak and report it to my folks, who would then have just another reason to be ashamed of me as not worthy of carrying on the tough Hannah tradition.

I even prayed to God for some answers, but I was so miserable, I really didn't even want Him inside, for fear He would see that I was not a steel-tough jock but rather the sensitive little kid I had been at 12 years old when my butt got whipped and then got chewed out by my dad. But I always knew deep down God loved me and would protect me when things became too much for me to handle. It wasn't until much later that I finally realized that my trying too hard to handle things was always what got me in trouble, and if I had trusted God more to guide me in all things, He would lead me in the ways that would honor Him first, and all the rest would follow.

As the first few weeks of school passed and we got into football schedules and classroom work, I buried that anger and homesickness and kept it hidden from anyone for the rest of my term at Baylor. I never actually got rid of it; I just buried it. As a coping mechanism, I established my identity early at Baylor with a fairly healthy—some would quickly call it cocky—ego, though I didn't fully appreciate just how big my head was already starting to be or how much more it would swell in the coming years. I also had no idea that same swollen head would be the primary cause of one of the first major failures of my life—my transferring away from Baylor at the end of my junior year.

Life at a military prep school meant extremely short haircuts, crisply pressed uniforms, spit-shined shoes, and exacting compliance with rules and regulations. None of those were familiar to me, and I quickly learned they were not my preferred way of being controlled. Many of the professors were former military members, and many of them had a penchant for ordering young guys around. One of them in particular was downright sadistic about it and used demeaning intimidation like a drill sergeant and meted out corporal punishment like making the cadets fall to their knees and put their hands under them, so one would be resting on his knuckles. He was also big on making them drop and do 50 pushups as fast as they could or doing knee lifts until they collapsed. I would soon become the focus of his anger and need to control me. Others like Major Luther Worsham, however, exerted authority and discipline with an encouraging and healthy attitude with the goal of molding young men into productive adults of strong character and moral discipline. A couple of the other professors were also football or track coaches, and I actually developed an amount of respect and affection for them. I remained wary and somewhat distrustful of anyone except Maj. Worsham.

He was one exceptional teacher/coach who became somewhat of a father figure to me. He reminded me so much of my own father—both in stature and demeanor—and because he knew I really wanted to learn from him ways to make myself a better athlete and person. Major Luther T. "Luke" Worsham Jr., or simply "The Maj," was a stocky and strong former Army major who had seen combat in World War II, fought in the African campaign, and returned home with both skin cancer and a head of snow white hair. It prematurely turned that color because of the unspeakable harshness of endless days under the African sun and the ungodly stresses of the war. A married father of two girls, he walked with a confident strut, shoulders squarely held, and with his jaw firmly set. Until his death a couple of years ago, Maj still wore his snow white hair in a high and tight Marine cut, and his forearms remained thick and firm as fence posts. Oddly he had a somewhat high and shrilly voice that we guessed was brought on by his constant yelling. In the indoor training rooms, he always wore sleeveless gray flannel sweatshirts, and outside he always wore a wide-brimmed straw hat to protect against the sun's harsh rays. His wife, Betty Flo, or "Miss Flo" as we students referred to her, was one of the sweetest, kindest people I have ever met, and she was also like a surrogate mother to me the entire time I was at Baylor.

Most students respected Maj. Worsham because, in addition to being an enthusiastic teacher in the biology classroom and a hands-on motivator of student-athletes on the field and wrestling mat, Maj. Worsham was no stranger to dishing immediate—and I mean lightning quick—corporal punishment to a student caught misbehaving. His reprimands were usually delivered swiftly, surely, and without warning. Maj. Worsham would give a quick yank of a handful of hair or plant his size-10 boot swiftly up against a backside. He could bark orders, criticism, and encouragement equally well with a drill sergeant's command and precision. And, he was loud, too, even with that oddly shrill voice…especially on the football field where he became my offensive blocking and techniques coach from Day One.

I first met Maj. Worsham when I attended an introductory camp during the summer before my freshman year. But my first *true* introduction to Maj. Worsham was on the military drill field. On one occasion early on, I was goofing off with one of my buddies in my platoon and I didn't realize Maj. Worsham was behind us. He caught us, came straight up to me, grabbed a hank of my hair, and literally pulled me up off the ground. I was standing there suspended on my tiptoes trying to reach his hand the best I could, and he's hollering in my ear with that real shrill voice he had: "You goofball! What are you, a jackass? Are you going to take this seriously, or am I going to have to pull every hair out of your scalp?" All I could do was stutter, "Yes, sir! Yes, sir! Yes, sir!" That was my first introduction to a man who would become a very important figure in my life, and it made quite an impression on me.

From then on, I listened to him very carefully and took a great interest in the many lessons he would teach me—lessons in life that stay with me to this day. My next interaction with him was later in the fall when I went out for the wrestling team. Maj. Worsham was with one of the other coaches in the old wrestling gym, which was always heated to about 90 degrees or more. I told him I wanted to try out for the wrestling team. He came straight over to me again like he did when I acted up in drill formation, grabbed me by the elbow, pulled me to the middle of the mat, and threw me on my side. Quick as a cat, he jumped on me and sank a half-nelson hold on me, and crammed my face right up in his nasty, sweaty armpit.

My nose was literally buried up in his armpit, and I couldn't breathe. I was sucking wind like I was dying, and it felt like he was about to break my neck. I knew in that second he was one tough, old bird and strong as an ox and I quit struggling. And just like that, he let me go and said, "That's how you do it. *That's* how you do it." So in the first two minutes of trying out for the wrestling team, I learned how to do a half-nelson hold. As a matter of fact after that first lesson under Maj. Worsham, the half-nelson became my favorite pin move because I knew how it felt, and I figured if I could ever get a guy in a half-nelson, he would just give up like I did.

I made the team and went on to wrestle heavyweight my sophomore and junior years. I went on to win the state heavyweight title my junior year. Though I loved the sport, Maj. Worsham made us work and he worked us hard. But the thing I always realized and every kid knew was that Maj. Worsham loved the boys just like they were his sons. If a kid put his heart into trying to learn and improve and worked hard at it, Maj. Worsham was on that kid's side. And even though he worked you and would discipline you if you gave less than 100 percent, kind of like God the Father, you always knew deep down that he had your best interests at heart. And just as I learned those first two minutes into trying out, he was hands-on in demonstrating techniques, whether on the wrestling mat, in the classroom, or out on the track and football fields.

He was also a great track coach, and naturally since I was a big kid, he encouraged me to go out for track and field, specifically to throw the shot put and discus, which he taught me how to do. The other baseball coaches wanted me to try out that spring for catcher, but since I couldn't hit or throw a curveball, I opted for track. In addition Maj. Worsham also pointed out a couple of things that might make me a better athlete all the way around, and I wanted to work with him that spring. First he saw that I was duck-footed, and that when I ran I didn't have a very long stride. He started working to help me with that by showing me two drills. After I would finish throwing the shot put and working with the discus, he would have me run the lines on the football field. He made me put both my feet directly on the hash mark and started me walking on it—kind of like a field sobriety test. When I got the hang of that, I started running it. His whole idea was to stop me from putting my heel on the line and splaying my toes outside to the left of it. It was heel, toe, heel, toe. He made me stay right on the line, and as I practiced that first drill more and more, eventually I stopped walking duck-footed. With his help and insight, I actually trained myself to walk almost pigeon-toed, which greatly improved my speed and stride when I ran at full speed.

The other thing he did was have me run the high hurdles. There are three steps between each hurdle, and what it forced you to do is lengthen your stride even more. I think it took me about three or four weeks just to get across two hurdles—much less all of them. But I was finally able to run the entire distance jumping those high hurdles, and that drill not only lengthened my stride but also improved my speed significantly. Developing that kind of fast, straight-line speed is something for which I owe Maj. Worsham. Without those drills he put me through, I would have never reached the level I did. Although I didn't know it at the time, Maj. Worsham was also thinking ahead to football season because these improvements came in handy in the fall. When he was my offensive line coach, he improved my speed and stride to push me beyond anything I could have imagined.

As I adjusted to the rigors of military boarding school, Maj. Worsham's intense interest in me was something I craved. Despite his disciplined exterior, I think he could see right into my soul and sense the real me that occupied my otherwise formidable body. In fact I know he could because in one of our earliest eye-to-eye exchanges, his blue eyes twinkled with a knowing appreciation of the sensitive, inner child, which was hiding inside me, and I felt him telegraphing me a mental clue that he could identify with the real me. I think he had a similar inner child who remained in hiding even after all his years in the war and despite the tough military exterior and persona he adopted thereafter.

Maj. Worsham and a couple of other coaches made two great big barge ropes. We were to climb those ropes every day. You were supposed to climb it, touch the top, and shimmy back down. It was meant to develop upper body strength. This other guy, Alex Roberts, was a great wrestler and a good football player, but he just didn't have the size to play in the league we were in. Alex had a set of six-pack abs, though, and it was just unbelievable how strong he was. He could actually climb the rope by pushing as well as pulling himself up. On the other hand, I was fat and weak and I couldn't climb the dang thing. I would get so far up and couldn't go any farther and would fall back down. But the first time I climbed the rope all the way to the top was during Christmas vacation my junior year and I was staying in Chattanooga with Alex. He was an officer and in a military prep school, and officers were allowed to carry actual swords. One day after practice, we were climbing the rope and I got about half to three-quarters of the way up when all of sudden I felt weak and started to let go. Then I felt the tip of a sword up my butt, and Alex was standing under me saying, "All the way, all the way, *all* the way, Hannah!" And Maj. Worsham was standing off to the side, laughing as hard as he could. With that cold steel aimed right at my derriere, that was the first time I ever climbed the rope all the way to the top. After that I actually became pretty good at it despite my size and weight increasing significantly between my freshman and junior years.

All that being said, before I decided to write this book, I guess if there was ever a person in my early life that I thought I could totally trust with knowing the real me, it was Maj. When he talked, he was talking with me, not talking to me. And when he spoke with me, I listened. He could coach me, he could encourage me, he could lighten me up when I got too down, and he could sure fire me up when I was dragging. I truly loved that guy. If there was a single living soul other than my father who contributed the most lessons that helped me achieve what I did in the sports arena and the business world, it was Major Luther T. Worsham. He died on May 14, 2002, and besides the death of my own parents, it was one of the saddest days of my life.

Throughout my NFL career, I used many of the lessons Maj. Worsham taught me in my high school days. In the August 3,

1981 issue of *Sports Illustrated* which surprisingly declared me "The Best Offensive Lineman of All Time," the author, Paul Zimmerman, spoke of my giving credit to Maj. Worsham for helping me develop, among many other things, some valuable blocking techniques. Zimmerman wrote:

> Worsham taught him how to zero in on a target, to aim for the numbers with his helmet, to keep his eyes open and his tail low. Next came the quick feet. Forget about pass blocking if you can't dance. Worsham helped there, too.
>
> "Oddly enough," Hannah says, "he helped me develop agility and reactions by putting me on defense in a four-on-one drill. It was the most terrible thing in the world. If the guard blocked down, you knew you'd better close the gap and lower your shoulder. If the end came down and the guard came out, buddy, you grabbed dirt because you knew a trap was coming."

Those specific talents which enabled me to cross step or toe-dance left and right kind of separated me from most other guards in the pros because nobody else handled the line like that. I had to think like a defensive lineman, so I could anticipate him and then get the best of him. Another thing Maj. Worsham focused on—besides the fact I had grown to nearly 6'2" and 235 pounds by the end of my sophomore year—was the extraordinary length of my arms. When he excitedly first pointed out to me the fact that my arms were already 37 inches long at the end of that year, he told me "Hannah! You're a *freak*, boy! I have *never* seen—much less coached a lineman—with arms that long! If you work with me, I'll show you how to use those chimpanzee arms to block the passing rush where nobody's going to be able to get by you, boy!"

I, though, was no giant by professional football standards. When I finally hit 6'3" and nearly 270 pounds in 1972, many people thought drafting me was a mistake because I was too short. Those long arms Maj. Worsham noticed, however, were also taken into account by the scouts, who saw how I was able to use them in pass blocking better than a lot of other guards. My arms became two of my main weapons, and a number of critics became my supporters when they realized I could actually scratch my ankles without bending down. Patriots offensive line coach Red Miller would repeat Maj. Worsham's sentiments during my first year with New England. Coach Miller, too, told me that my arms were one of my main advantages in aggressively protecting the pass rush.

Maj. Worsham became someone I trusted, someone I loved, and someone I admired. My respect for him is indelible and unfathomable. As I didn't get to say a proper goodbye to him before he died, I want him to know now how very grateful I am that God let me share that time with him and I thank God abundantly for sharing him with me.

I also pray that God doesn't ask that stocky, white-haired man with the cut-off sweatshirt and sunhat what a half-nelson is.

CHAPTER 7

Fights, Suspensions, and Expulsion

A COUNSELOR IN BOSTON introduced me to the wisdom of the Enneagram and its fantastic utility as a key to introspective examination of what personality type you most likely are. The Enneagram is an ancient theory and descriptive term drawn from the Greek word *ennea*, or nine, and gram, which simply means picture. It is also a fundamental mathematical correlation of nine distinct personality types, which work in harmonious relationship with all the others in a perfect circle of life. The nine different personality types are given specific titles like the Reformer, the Helper, the Achiever, the Loyalist, etc.

The Enneagram is a critical sword to help us understand the true personality we were born with and helps us cut through the many layers of the impostor faces we all adopt to cope with our human existence. When used in conjunction with an immersion into God's word, it is a fascinating research tool that can help one reach much greater spiritual clarity. Having applied all of the principles of the Enneagram to myself, which is essentially a brutally honest, incisive test and examination of one's own behaviors and thoughts, I am unquestionably and indelibly...an eight or the Challenger.

The basic description of a type-eight personality is best summarized in the Don Riso and Russ Hudson book, *The Wisdom of the Enneagram:*

> ***The Challenger:*** The powerful, dominating type. Eights are self-confident, strong and assertive. Protective, resourceful and decisive, they can also be proud and domineering. Eights feel that they must control their environment, often becoming confrontational and intimidating. Eights typically have problems with allowing themselves to be closer to others. At their best, healthy Eight's are self-mastering—they use their strengths to improve other's lives, becoming heroic, magnanimously, and sometimes historically great...At their worst, they may become belligerent, defiant, and threatening as they desperately try to "stay in control at any cost."

Trying to "stay in control at any cost" and not let others push me around has gotten me in more trouble than anything else my entire life. That mind-set deepened after I entered Baylor School for Boys, and it was greatly responsible for my huge early failure: an angry exit from Baylor at the end of my junior year under circumstances that were partially self-inflicted and primarily forced on me by those who sought to control me the most...and who ultimately wanted to break me.

One particular critic of mine was an older professor, Colonel Watson, who had developed a thinly veiled if not open disdain for me. I still trusted my coaches—especially Major Worsham—to protect and defend me because I felt they would stand up to people like Col. Watson, who developed a personal vendetta against me. I believed Maj. Worsham would defend me if and when Watson would try to frustrate the athletic department by exercising extreme discipline on me—the coach's pet superstar.

I guess I was well-targeted by my third year, but in one memorable event, I was wrongfully and unreasonably disciplined for a harmless, junior prank on some freshmen cadets. A couple of other juniors and I had tossed our shoes in with some seniors' shoes, which was an accepted form of older classmates demeaning the new boys by making them shine our shoes before inspection. No physical coercion, hitting, or cursing was involved. And since I had been made to do it a number of times my freshman year, it was almost a tradition to pass it on down to the younger guys.

One of the younger guys, however, told an associate of Col. Watson's, Ray Deering, an exaggerated and worse version of what I had done, and Mr. Deering turned me in to the guidance committee for hazing. Well, even though I might have intimidated the younger kids to shine my shoes, I never laid a finger on any of them nor had I threatened them with harm. I got called up on charges for hazing nonetheless, and Col. Watson took it as another opportunity to target me. When Watson confronted me, I defended myself on the grounds that we weren't physically touching or hurting the boys, and it was a prank that every other junior had done in fun one time or another.

However, Col. Watson greatly resented the fact I was standing my ground and adamantly defending what I thought were unfair charges. I had already been on disorder and detention for prior demerits, which meant I couldn't leave the campus for any reason other than to go to church. And I was sick of being singled out more than anyone else on campus, especially for something so slight as this. But Watson began coming after me, boring in, calling me a bully and a coward, and then got right up in my face, and daring me, "C'mon! Pick on me, big boy, if you're so damn tough!"

Watson pushed me over the edge when he did that, and I snapped. I jumped up, fists clenched and veins popping out of my neck and yelled back at him in a roar: "Any fucking WHERE! ANY FUCKING TIME!"

I guess I shouldn't have done that.

I should have been expelled on the spot, but I wasn't. From then on I was irretrievably on Col. Watson's hit list. I began getting tons of demerits for not following strict rules. I was forced into study hall when everyone else was on free time. I found myself socially grounded and restricted from leaving the campus for a never-ending number of reasons, a lot of which I deserved, and some I absolutely did not. For these latter pile-ons, I became downright defiant and obstinate, daring the administration to punish as hard as they could in order to show them they would not break me no matter what punishment they delivered.

I was constantly on disorder and banned from leaving the campus, but it always was for two weeks at a time because if you got three consecutive weeks' disorder, you were prevented from playing on any athletic teams. But by then Baylor had developed a double standard with me because it would be unthinkable for its football team to not play one of its best athletes or for the wrestling team to lose its heavyweight contender—especially when Baylor was about to play its archrival across town, another military prep school called McCallie.

As with most other schools known for both excellence in education and sports, I began to believe there was a natural and often hostile tension between the pure academic professors and those teachers who were hired primarily as coaches. The academics seemed somewhat disdainful of the intellect and acumen of several coaches, whom the former mostly saw as impostor bully teachers of inferior intellect. Meanwhile, some coaches viewed the academicians as wimpy snobs who made up for their lack of physical prowess by enlarging their brains and egos. This, of course, wasn't the case with every teacher or coach.

Through the next three years, I also came to sense there was no small amount of jockeying and posturing between the two camps for the attention and financial support of the school's board of trustees, which was replete with successful and well-heeled, moneyed alumni. The tension between the two classes of teachers often clashed as the academics sought more financial support, recognition for educational excellence, and awards while the coaches sought funding for better equipment, more fields, and more publicity as the respective teams won games and earned titles. As most of the teachers in both camps were from military backgrounds, there were secret campaigns waged and strategies employed by either to achieve their goals. Sadly, an outstanding academic program or exceptional sports team might be used as a point of contention in a boardroom game of tug of war. As I also came to believe much later, there was certainly no lack of posturing in their respective attempts to thwart the other's efforts, often undertaken without regard for the best interests of students.

I guess when you really boil it down, it's an adult version of the high school clash between "jocks" and "nerds." Regardless, getting caught in the crossfire between those warring turfs could be very painful. I found that out as a junior and then again nearly 40 years later when God would lure me back to Baylor in a completely different capacity for an even harsher education.

Speaking out of both sides of its mouth, the Baylor administration was having its cake and eating it, too. On the one hand, the ones who didn't tolerate my "jock" mentality were reining me in and controlling me. At the same time, the coaches were able to use me to their full advantage against all comers in the athletic arena. I was being treated like an assault dog, who they sic on the opposition during games but is otherwise kept on a very short chain near the doghouse. Because I was restricted to campus, I lost any sense of freedom. I lost some good friends and I also lost my first girlfriend. But most of all, I lost total respect for authority—except what I still had for the coaches who consoled me in private with the main one being Maj. Worsham.

In the spring of that awful junior year, I had been on disorder nearly the entire time from the fall before, but I was nearing the end of my last week of disorder without any further infractions. If I completed that term, I would finally get to go into town. But one Sunday afternoon, Bill Bealer and I were caught by Col. Watson with mud all over our clothes, and I had no shoes on in the Quad after playing a game of touch football. We were simply waiting there for a few minutes for our girlfriends to bring us some snacks and drinks. Not wearing shoes in the Quad was a technical violation, and Col. Watson immediately gave me the choice of accepting one week of disorder or going before the guidance council. I wanted to take the one week instead of going before the guidance council as I didn't trust what they would do or how Watson might influence them otherwise.

But Mr. Harris, one of the advisors we consulted, convinced me that if I bowed to Col. Watson one more time and did not buck him, I would only get two hours of study hall from the guidance council, and it would be over. I agreed to do what Harris suggested. When the findings of the guidance council were announced on Thursday of the following week by Sgt. Joe Key, my buddy, Bill Bealer, only got two hours of study hall, but when my name was called, I got two more weeks of disorder. I totally lost it.

I was now behind the proverbial eight ball. My "eight" personality caught up with me, and I regressed into the worst part of my character. I felt I had been completely misled—basically set up—by Mr. Harris. I knew from then on that I could never trust anyone ever again except maybe Maj. Worsham and my dad. After that utter disaster, I simply quit caring about anything and took the two additional weeks of disorder. During that time I began smoking a lot of cigarettes and drinking beer and generally acting like a total ass. I just didn't care anymore, and because of my terrible attitude, everyone knew it.

When I was almost at the end of that last two-week disorder, I was finally going to get to go into town for the first time of my entire junior year. With only a couple more days to go, I was standing in the commissary line behind all these seventh and eighth graders, waiting for my turn to buy a soda and snack. A sophomore who also played football, Rex Yon, suddenly broke in line in front of me and all the others. Yon was a lineman, too, and a big one at that—only an inch or so shorter than I was, and he probably weighed about 210. His cutting in line really got to me because Yon was one of the day school guys who held a grudge against me. Earlier that year after summer break, Yon had showed up and let his hair grow into one of those Goldilocks, surfer boy looks. I was one of the guys who was supposed to lead the linemen, and if any player on the team did not keep their hair short and trim, we would all be punished.

I wasn't going to let that happen. When a couple of us cornered him behind the gym and told him to cut his hair, so we wouldn't all be punished, he basically said, "Screw you." He shouldn't have done that because those two other guys and I jumped him behind the athletics building, held him down, and forcibly cut his hair off. Yon hated me from then on.

So when he jumped in front of me and all the other kids, I called him out. Yon, however, just started taunting me, and I instantly thought, *Uh Oh…what have I done?* Yon probably knew I was very close to ending my disorder and finally getting to go into town, so he probably bet that I would just stand there and take his lip instead of fighting him. Another fight would probably leave me on disorder for the rest of the year or probably get me kicked out of school completely. I had to stand there in front of all the other younger guys and back down from the fight Yon was clearly picking.

He, however, kept on jawing at me. I tried to move away from him, telling him that I was *not* going to fight him. I was *not* going to get kicked out of school. I moved to three different soda machines, keeping my back to him the entire time. My anger was to the point of rage. My jaws were clenched and grinding enamel from my molars. My heart was pounding fiercely as I struggled to keep control of myself and fought the surging adrenaline and the instinct to turn around and tear into him.

Yon, however, called me a son of a bitch in front of all those other, younger kids, and no one calls my mom that. When he yelled that, I just went blind. I balled my fist up, wheeled around with a full haymaker, and hit him as hard as I possibly could square in the mouth and nose. I had been working out extra hard that spring with the 12-pound shot put for the track team, and my 37-inch right arm had gained a frightening amount of additional strength that surprised even me. I don't remember hitting him at all. The next thing I knew, I saw him lying on the ground in a dark crimson pool with blood gushing out of his mouth and nose, and I said, "Oh, my God, I've killed him."

I had broken his jaw and knocked out several teeth.

The aftermath of hurting Yon so badly was a blur. He was from a well-to-do family who were part of the Baylor upper crust, and they wanted me expelled immediately. The administration basically told me later that I wasn't exactly kicked out, but one more infraction, and I would be expelled *permanently*. It was kind of like being on double-secret probation like those fraternity guys from *Animal House*. No matter what they did, they eventually would be goners. The fact I wasn't immediately expelled was of little consolation as I knew it was just a matter of time. With little counsel or advice, I thought long and hard about it and simply left Baylor.

■ | | | | ■

I felt frustrated, disgusted, and totally betrayed. I wondered why Maj. Worsham didn't fight to keep me as I hoped he would. He probably did, but as long as Col. Watson and others like him still controlled Baylor, none of the coaches had enough pull to actually overrule them or protect me. That meant there was really nobody who could look out for me. Those in power would certainly find a way to ultimately kick me out anyway.

What really cinched the decision for me to leave Baylor after three long years was the thought—or fear—that if I did stay and try to finish my senior year I would ultimately get expelled. And that would ruin any chance I might have at getting a scholarship at any of the major programs, which had shown interest in me.

I thought it through a million times and prepared my speech for my folks and delivered it with conviction. Even though Dad understood and acquiesced, the decision I made was worsened when I later realized how utterly disappointed he actually was. I think he saw that I was just running away from my problems instead of facing them head on. Over time I realized Dad was right, but I truly believe that Dad forgave me for having tarnished the opportunity he gave me. But that wound would not truly be healed until many years later when he was given the honor of introducing me into the Pro Football Hall of Fame in 1991. Then I fully realized what a truly wonderful and amazingly supportive father he was to me all my life.

During the weeks and months after I left Baylor, the only thing I could think about was how much I had failed and how badly I had disappointed my two dads: Herb Hannah and Maj. Worsham. I asked God to forgive me over and over, but somehow I never quite got the reassurance in my soul that I had done things correctly or honored Him in the process. I found myself praying for forgiveness and for letting Him down.

From that horrendous failure at age 17, I reaffirmed the distrust in almost everyone and the deep-rooted fear of being controlled like that again...by anyone. I became firmly convinced that I had been betrayed by everyone I had ever relied on, except my dad and Maj. Worsham. My mind-set became: *Even if you succeed, people are going to turn against you. But if you push it to the limit and stand your ground, then maybe, just maybe you can win back—or take their approval and respect.*

I turned my back on Baylor and went back home to finish my senior year in Albertville, Alabama. Even though I was immediately recognized as a top football player as a senior, the mix of anger and guilt I had about not finishing at Baylor left the accolades feeling pretty hollow. The college scouts, though, did take notice, and when they started visiting Albertville that year to check me out, the University of Alabama was among the first.

CHAPTER 8

Bama Comes Calling

ALBERTVILLE, ALABAMA, IS 150 miles northeast of Tuscaloosa, the home of the University of Alabama and its powerhouse Crimson Tide football program. College football in Alabama is a pastime reveled in by princes and paupers alike, and the loyalty and rabidity of the fans who support the Crimson Tide football team, and its cross-state rival, the Auburn Tigers, is a passion of the highest and most extreme degree. Football is the great equalizer in Alabama, and all that matters is that you cheer for either Alabama or Auburn. The seriousness of the rivalry between these two major SEC football programs in our state is colossal, and sometimes downright vicious. In the late summer and early fall in Alabama, it is said the colors of the changing leaves on Alabama's trees turn deep crimson and even a little orange and blue the farther south you go.

The tradition and lore of the mighty playing legends and past teams of Alabama Tide football is a way of life in this wonderful Southern state nestled deep in the Heart of Dixie. Cars, SUVs, and trucks, which sport an Alabama crimson "A" seem to outnumber those which don't. The challenge to come up with another automobile vanity license plate to relay school support for the Tide—such as TSH4UA or ROLETYD—is something more than a few thousand fans are willing to pay the extra fee for year in and year out. The state tax coffers are helped substantially by the Tide or Auburn fans who want a vanity license plate that swears allegiance to their respective team. The Auburn fans who enjoy the same challenge are equally motivated to show their colors and creativity on their bumper stickers, and depending on where you are in the state, one side usually outnumbers the other.

I was never the least interested in playing for Auburn. I had made up my mind. If I didn't get a scholarship to Tuscaloosa but Auburn offered a full ride, I was going across the state line to play for Georgia because my mom had taught there, and we used to root for Georgia all the time—except when they played Alabama. Although I was born and raised a Tide fan, I rooted for Auburn when it was playing anyone other than Georgia. I know it sounds odd, but when our major rival was playing most other teams especially those in the SEC, I rooted for the state of Alabama's football teams, and an Auburn win against an SEC opponent would make the stakes even higher when Alabama played the same team. College football is a way of life in Alabama, and now that the Tide is on a streak with three national titles in four years and no telling how many more in the coming years, I think the rest of the country is catching on, too.

The University of Alabama campus sits in the heart of Tuscaloosa and sprawls outward more and more as the school has grown. The academic buildings, dorms, and fraternity and sorority houses ring a beautifully preserved open lawn area called simply "the Quad." Most schools and universities have a quad of some sort—as did my military prep school at Baylor—but the Quad in Tuscaloosa is something special. It is anchored by a tall carillon, Denny Chimes, which has become representative of the entire school, and the tolling of the bells from the old tower swell the nostalgia and school fealty in any Crimson Tide fan who has ever walked the campus. The tower is also within close eyeshot of Bryant-Denny stadium, now the crucible of Crimson Tide football after years of Alabama's bigger home football games against opponents like Tennessee, LSU, and Ole Miss being played 54 miles to the northeast at the old Legion Field in Birmingham.

That kind of fervor has coursed through the veins of football fans in Dixie forever, and as coach Paul "Bear" Bryant had led Bama to several national championships and SEC titles throughout the '60s, I was determined to play for him and hopefully make a serious contribution to the team. As I returned to Albertville, Alabama, to play football my final year in high school, I returned to my blood red roots and played my heart out for Albertville High School, consciously wondering every single game if there were Alabama football scouts there watching the game and watching me in particular. It wasn't long until I learned they were...and not for just one game or two. And, yes, I did indeed learn they were there looking specifically at me.

My coach learned through some fans in the stands that the very same scouts, who had come to see me play at Baylor in Chattanooga, Tennessee, my sophomore and junior years, were regularly visiting Albertville High football games many Friday nights of my senior year. As spring and graduation approached, I was invited twice—the maximum number of visits allowed by a recruit—to visit Tuscaloosa by those scouts, but Coach Bryant never came to my house. I had also been pursued by the University of Georgia, which was specifically looking to beef up its offensive line roster, and other SEC teams had also expressed interest in me, but I had made it fairly well known that the only choices I was interested in were Bama, Georgia, and USC. I looked hard at USC because at the time it was a dynasty program and I wanted to play at the highest level I could to strengthen my chances for a shot in the pro draft. My Uncle Bill Hannah, who played at Alabama, had also coached at California State University, Fullerton before he died in a plane crash on November 13, 1971 with two other coaches, Joe O'Hara and Dallas Moon. So I had a sense of honor about giving USC a fair shake. But it was mighty far from Albertville, and even though the Trojans were a major powerhouse football program, I focused on Alabama.

Dad, however, sat me down and said, "Son, you can go anywhere you want to, but you have to ask yourself one simple question: When you come back home from anywhere other than Alabama, where do you think you are going to eat?" He kind of chuckled, but deep down, I knew he was serious. He had played at Bama after World War II, and later on, my Uncle Bill actually played there for Coach Bryant as well. The blood in our house was crimson. Dad reminded me that when I was in the third grade, I already loved Alabama football so much and really wanted an actual Alabama football to throw around that he urged me to write a letter to Coach Bryant. To my great surprise, this box arrived in the mail a couple of weeks later, and in it was a personally autographed football from Coach Bryant. I never actually played with the ball because he had signed it, of course, but it still remains one of my all time favorite pieces of sports memorabilia.

I remained interested in playing for Georgia, and coach Vince Dooley, himself, actually talked to me about playing for the Bulldogs a couple of times. He and his staff put a full-court press on me and offered a full ride scholarship for all four years if I would commit to play for the Bulldogs. I thought hard about it mainly because Mom had taught there and she was a big fan, but deep down I knew my heart and future college career would most likely be playing for the Alabama Crimson Tide. Dad was fairly persuasive in at least having me consider those two options of Georgia and Alabama, but in the end, if Bama came through with the same full ride, it was clear as crystal that he wanted me to sign with the Tide. He didn't outright order me to choose Alabama, but my making cracks like—"Where I was going to eat?"—when I came home from some other school, his encouragement to select the Crimson Tide was less than subtle.

Before I signed for the University of Alabama, Coach Bryant never once visited my home and family in Albertville, though he did visit other high school recruits in Alabama and around the country. As I came to learn, Bryant's penchant for coaxing the top defensive players was his priority, but I was still among a small number of guys he invited down to Tuscaloosa for a second visit, and we were taken into the A Club Room, the crucible of Alabama athletics where many of the trophies and pictures of former star players, teams, and coaches are displayed. Coach Bryant went around and shook everybody's hands and then gave a short recruiting speech to us. "Boys, I am sure a lot of other teams are offering you scholarships and other things to play for them, but if you really want to be a *champion*, Alabama is where you want to come."

That was it, short and sweet...and totally convincing. I promised myself and my folks that if I ever did get the chance to play for the Bear I would show him and everyone else what a great player I could become.

■ | | | | ■

There is an aura, a mystique which surrounds Alabama football, and gameday in Tuscaloosa is an event that rarely has equal anywhere else in the SEC. The 100,000-plus loyal fans who begin gathering there sometimes four days before big home games (to snag one of the prime RV parking spots or to secure a key place on the Quad for tailgating, grilling, socializing, and drinking) are loyal and fanatic down to every last corpuscle of their Crimson blood. It's no small testament to the draw of Bama football that even when the team plays an intra-squad game, the stadium is packed with more than 92,000 screaming fans. Houndstooth fedora hats are a noted trademark for men, women, and kids alike, which remain a venerable nod to the trademark chapeau worn by the Tide's most revered former coach, Bryant. Other less favored headgear, but equally as noticeable, are worn by the few brave souls who dare don a box of Tide laundry detergent and a roll of white toilet paper taped to it, as a symbolic version of the Bama cheer "Roll Tide! Roll" yelled in unison by every fan in the stadium as our place kicker prepares to send the ball to the opposing team.

Since coach Nick Saban has been at the helm of the Crimson Tide team, Alabama has returned to the apex of the NCAA program and remains a perennial threat to claim yet another national title. After Coach Bryant died (shortly after retiring in 1982 and claiming his 315th career win) the only head coach since him, who earned even a degree of time-honored respect before Saban came along, was Gene Stallings, the gravelly-voiced Texan who led Bama to the national title in 1992. After Stallings' tenure other coaches came and went, and the Alabama program sank into mediocrity, at best.

Now most Alabama fans see Mal Moore, the athletic director who lured Saban, as a genius, a hero, and perhaps a savior of some sort. Saban is now the highest paid head college football coach in the country, and any Bama fan you meet will tell you he is worth every penny and more. Some folks have even started a rumble that the stadium in Tuscaloosa is destined to be renamed Saban-Bryant-Denny stadium any day now. That any other coach would ever again command the adoration and respect of the fans and administration like Coach Bryant did was once unthinkable. But, now…well, there's a new idol in Tuscaloosa, and his name is Nick. Some even call him *Saint* Nick.

CHAPTER 9

Playing for the Bear

AFTER I WAS offered the full ride scholarship, I signed with Alabama a few days later. I was following in the footsteps of some amazing players who will be forever immortalized in the annals of football, names like—Bart Starr, Joe Namath, Steve Sloan, Ray Perkins, Jackie Sherrill, Kenny Stabler, Tommy Tolleson, Lee Roy Jordan, Paul Crane, and Steve Bowman. I also had some pretty awesome teammates, including fellow guards Buddy "Bearcat" Brown, Jim Krapf, Steve Sprayberry, and quarterback Scott Hunter, and our own "Italian Stallion" Johnny Musso, the fiery running back who still stands near the top of the all-time best running backs the school has ever had.

Wilbur Jackson, a rising superstar in the backfield along with Musso, started in my senior year, and in my opinion, those two guys were the hardest charging, strongest halfbacks who played the game during those years. I also had the great privilege of playing under some awesome assistant coaches, including (future athletic director) Mal Moore, (future Auburn coach) Pat Dye, Bill Oliver, Richard Williamson, John David

Crowe, Dude Hennessey, Sam Bailey, and my offensive line coach, Jeremy Sharpe.

It was an interesting time to be playing for the Alabama Crimson Tide, and from the outset, I was determined to be among the best the team had ever seen. Until I became part of the program, I didn't realize that Coach Bryant was a defense-oriented coach. Turns out he was quoted as saying, "If they can't score on you, the worst you can do is end up in a tie." He always assigned his best players to the defense, and when I came on board, that's where he slotted me. However, for reasons I'm unclear about, Sharpe talked privately with Coach Bryant and somehow got me moved to the right side of the ball.

Freshmen were not allowed to play their first year, so I had to sit on the sidelines in 1969. We were still required to maintain minimum academic standards, and I learned a funny lesson early in my freshman year when I had to write my first English essay. Having gone to a prep school like Baylor, I had been taught to write in the traditional style of the King's English. When I turned in that first paper, my professor commented that my writing style was too stiff and formal, so I should loosen it up a bit. I decided right then I would do just enough schoolwork to remain academically eligible to play and kind of slide through the rest of my studies, which I did for the rest of the time I was at Alabama. I could focus better on football, and that's what I was really at Alabama to do anyway. So I spent most of my freshman time getting to know the team, the coaches, and the drills.

Our 1969 season—and my freshman season—ended with a 6–5 record, including disappointing losses to Vanderbilt (14–10), Tennessee (41–14), LSU (20–15), Auburn (49–26), and Colorado (47–33 in the Liberty Bowl).

But I also learned a lot about the way Coach Bryant led his team, players, and coaches. He was someone who you just naturally wanted to please, but someone you also knew could be tough as nails if you slacked off or did something boneheaded on or off the field. I don't know what was really at the core of his persona that drew people to him or inspired so many players to give it their all, but you'll hear so many fans and former players refer to him as a "member of the family" or "like my dad, uncle, or grandfather." He was someone you do not want to disappoint—especially if you had a chance to excel and actually earn praise from him.

I frankly don't think he was real excited about focusing too much on offensive linemen, and like I said, he never personally came to visit me or my folks before I committed to Alabama. But maybe—just maybe, if given a chance, I could work hard enough to impress him into treating me more than a piece of meat that cleared the way for our quarterbacks or running backs. Although I saw his great coaching style on display with so many other more important players, I always felt that he saw the front linesmen as low men on the totem pole, and he let someone else work one on one with them.

During my second year in 1970, I finally got to play for Alabama, but our record remained a very tepid 6–5–1 with a crushing 33–28 loss to Auburn, and I remember being as depressed as I've ever been from a loss. I also think the entire team became greatly disheartened. I began drinking a lot. I smoked way too many cigarettes. I got in arguments and fights more often than I care to remember. In general I adopted a surly attitude.

I also have to confess now that those years at Alabama were somewhat tumultuous in a completely different way. As my recognition and acclaim on the field grew, so did my ego. Off-field scuffles and troubles were not uncommon for me and a few of the other guys. A few of us, who grew a big head, drank too much and then drove from Tuscaloosa across the Mississippi line to Columbus, Mississippi, where there was a girls' school and a couple of bars where rival Mississippi State football players hung out. We ended up in a fight with them and left just in time to avoid getting arrested. We weren't really bad guys at all. We were just feeling our oats. The majority of the team and coaches were all pretty decent people, so our occasional misbehavior was really not that bad in the grand scheme of things or compared to what you read about these days with some teams having a bunch of outright thugs and criminals on the squad.

Even with all the talented players and excellent coaches, those years at Alabama from 1968 to 1970 saw a regrettable slump of Crimson Tide football from the heights it had reached with their national championship in 1961 and back-to-back national championship teams of 1964 and 1965. Many sportswriters and observers credit the regression of the Alabama program to the SEC's overall slowness in accepting integration and not allowing extremely talented African American players to participate fully in their football programs. Except for one black player, our 1970 Alabama team was all white.

When the 1970 football season rolled around, we were coming off that so-so 1969 season of 6–5, Coach Bryant's worst won-loss record yet. We were playing our opener against USC, which had lost only two games in three seasons, and we had our work cut out for us. USC was tough, very physical, and extremely fast. USC also had a roster of black players who were unbelievable. One of those guys was a running back, Sam "Bam" Cunningham, who would go on to be my teammate with the New England Patriots. The game at Legion Field was Cunningham's first road trip and his first game starting on the varsity.

The Trojans killed us. I mean they absolutely mauled the Tide and handed us a 42–21 trouncing that was downright embarrassing. They racked up 559 total yards—300 more than Bama—and Cunningham ran for 135 of those and scored two touchdowns in only 12 carries. It was humiliating beyond words. It became rumored that Coach Bryant had invited Sam into the Tide locker room and paraded him around, saying, "Boys, this is what a *real* football player looks like." Cunningham disputed that quote as an exaggeration, but he did tell me that Coach Bryant actually sought him out after the game and congratulated him on his performance. That rout of Bama by USC in 1970 became infamously known as the "Cunningham Game." Many said that 60 minutes on the field that did more to integrate Alabama than Martin Luther King Jr. did in 20 years.

As far as I am concerned, I truly believe Coach Bryant orchestrated that game in order for the South, especially Alabama, to break some mind-sets that African Americans didn't belong on the football field. I'm positive he knew there were African Americans recruited out of Alabama to play in other conferences and I'm also positive he knew there were some extraordinary black athletes in Alabama high schools that would make excellent players at Alabama if society would just accept it. That week we had a practice from a hell, which was an absolutely, grueling conditioning session. Part of me wonders if Bryant did that to intentionally wear us down before playing USC. I have no doubts that Coach Bryant was willing to risk a loss in that season just in order to possibly build a platform for a stronger team in the future—one that would include black players.

Well, that was Bryant's style and talent as a coach and a leader. He knew you couldn't intimidate players into playing better. You had to make them want to play better. It was the same way with integration and bringing black guys into the football picture at Alabama. You had to make people want to integrate teams, and Coach Bryant bringing Sam back into that locker room and saying, "Now here's what a *real* football player looks like," may have been a pure stroke of genius. And just as the state was on the brink of doing the right thing to totally integrate, it did need some coaxing, and I am morally convinced this game changed even a lot of hard-core redneck resisters' minds about putting black guys on the team. Like me, there's a great number of good Christians who realize the color of a man's skin is not what he is, but it's his spirit and what he is as a person that defines him at the core.

Not long after that game and the marginal 1970 season, things started to change in Alabama's football program in a big way, and Coach Bryant had to make some very crucial decisions. He was getting a lot of pressure from the university's administration and top private boosters to do something to turn things around and get the Tide back on a winning platform. Our fans were becoming depressed and disgruntled. You could hear the lack of enthusiasm in the stadiums. The players were somewhat lackadaisical, and team spirit was nearing an all-time low. There were rumblings among fans and boosters that maybe Coach Bryant had let the game of football pass him by and he had lost his effectiveness as a head coach. Alabama ended the 1970 season with a 24–24 tie against Oklahoma in the Astro-Bluebonnet Bowl, a mid-level bowl game. We had previously gotten skunked at Tennessee 24–0, then lost 14–9 to LSU in a squeaker, and lost again to Auburn 33–28, so I really don't think we cared much as a team whether we won or lost to Oklahoma. When we missed a field goal for the win, the boring tie simply underscored the lack of Crimson Tide fever.

Something changed about Coach Bryant that year. His edge just wasn't the same. He often appeared to be very lost in deep thought or focused on something only he could see. He didn't smile as much and he was quieter than ever before. Obviously, he had something really big on his mind, and many speculated whether he was contemplating giving it all up and quitting.

■ | | | | ■

While Alabama went into spring training in 1971 working the same pro-style passing offense plan it had used since the early 1960s, Coach Bryant had privately decided Bama just couldn't win anymore by mainly throwing the ball. According to coach Mal Moore, who replaced the departing Steve Sloan as Bama's quarterbacks coach, Bryant was impressed by the wishbone offense Oklahoma had run during that Bluebonnet Bowl.

With no fanfare or publicity, Coach Bryant went to see his old friends, Darrell Royal and Emory Bellard, at the University of Texas to learn about the extremely potent wishbone offense they had unveiled in 1968, and which Oklahoma, the archrival of the Longhorns, had adopted in 1970 under Sooners coach Chuck Fairbanks. When Texas introduced the wishbone at the opening of the 1968 season, the Longhorns sputtered to life and then took off, guns-a-blazing by tying their first game, losing the second, and then winning the next 30 straight games and two national championships. Some sportswriters actually credit Oklahoma with perfecting the wishbone. Oklahoma tallied the all-time NCAA rushing average in the '71 season with nearly 473 yards, a record which still stands.

Royal and Bellard spent a good portion of the summer of 1971 explaining the new offense to Coach Bryant, and after spending that time in Texas, Coach Bryant became convinced. He invited both Texas coaches to Tuscaloosa in late July to speak at a coaching clinic. Bellard's clinic was held in a hotel meeting room, and Moore, Sharpe, and running backs coach

Crow spent three full days learning the wishbone offense from Bellard and Royal.

Basically the wishbone was designed to give the offense three different options against rushing defensive linemen. Once the ball is snapped and the play is executed, one of the two running backs and the quarterback become additional blockers for the player who received the handoff or throw. For a team with some excellent short-yardage backs with enough muscle and speed like Musso and Jackson, we could pound away on the ground and make steady gains, which would add up overall into many more potential first downs and points.

Except for the quarterbacks and running backs who Coach Bryant had been working with late in the summer, the rest of our team didn't know a thing about the decision to convert to the wishbone offense until we reported to camp three weeks or so before practice began for the 1971 season. Our opener was again against USC, and we were going to play the Trojans at the Coliseum in Los Angeles. We learned the wishbone in total secrecy, so when we played in public practices we always showed the old pro-style passing offense. Even on the day before the Friday opener with USC, we still ran the old offense in our last practice in the Coliseum and never once showed the wishbone formation. Many sportswriters later commented that the strategy of springing the wishbone on USC was the "best kept secret in America." I liked the new offense. It wasn't all that hard to learn, and the team had a whole new level of excitement as we were learning new weapons to try and return Alabama to national glory. There was something especially exciting that we were practicing the wishbone in secret, and that brought the team a lot closer, too.

We beat Southern Cal 17–10 with our new offense. The next week we whipped Southern Miss 42–6 and then Florida 38–0.

We won against Vanderbilt 42–0 and then beat Tennessee 32–15. The streak continued as we trounced Houston, Mississippi State, LSU, Miami and then our biggest rival, Auburn, by a score of 31–7. We ended the regular season 11–0 and were selected to play against Nebraska in the Orange Bowl on January 1, 1972. As we approached the gridiron duel with one of the greatest powerhouse programs in the country with the national championship on the line, I considered that game the defining game of my college career.

I was unbelievably keyed up the night before the Orange Bowl, knowing we were going up against Nebraska, one of the giants of the college football world and one of the strongest, biggest, and toughest defensive programs in the land. We had practiced hard right before the game, and the entire team was pumped. I mean *pumped*. I couldn't sleep at all in the Miami hotel the night before. So at about midnight, I was just sitting on a bench by the elevators out in the lobby. I had my hands clutched, my head down, and was restlessly moving my legs to try and calm my nerves. Suddenly, the elevator door dinged and...out reeled Coach Bryant.

It caught me totally off guard and startled me into an adrenaline rush that shot my heart rate up to 100 or better. In an instant I realized he was drunk as he lurched through the doors. He caught sight of me sitting there on the bench and then did the unthinkable.

He stumbled over and plopped down next to me, smelling of whiskey and cigarettes. He leaned back against the wall, rolled his head over at me, and muttered, "John, you doing okay?" Then he stared at me, trying to get a better focus on who or what it is he's looking at. Unfortunately, such a look often turns into a glare—or at least what looks like a glare to somebody who is not equally drunk—and I was obviously totally sober before this huge bowl game against Nebraska. "Yes, sir," I replied. "I'm just keyed up and can't sleep. That's all." He rolled his head back and tilted it back until he was resting it against the wall and closed his eyes with a huge sigh. I thought, *Oh, Lord, he's going to go to sleep right here beside me,* and my mind began to race as I wondered what in the world I could possibly do to prevent this from becoming a huge disaster especially if someone else like a random hotel guest might happen to get off the next elevator.

As panic began to set in, he suddenly snapped up, looked at me, and then put both his hands on his knees with another huge sigh. He forced himself to stand up and said, "Okay, John, see if you can get some rest now, okay?" He then stumbled off and disappeared into the adjoining hall.

Unfortunately, the next day Nebraska handed us our only loss of the season in a spectacular thrashing in the Orange Bowl when they absolutely mauled us 38–6, a loss I still feel to this day. We went into that game ranked No. 2 in the country with a perfect 11–0 record and huge wins to our credit especially the big one against Auburn. Our confidence was high, but some private doubts persisted about whether we could continue to successfully run the new wishbone offense against a defensive monster like Nebraska. Maybe we were a bit too cocky despite those doubts. Maybe we just peaked too early. Frankly, those Cornhuskers was simply too intimidating, and we came up woefully short on our execution and delivery. That 38–6 loss was Coach Bryant's worst loss of his career. And it was the last game I ever played for Coach Bryant and Alabama.

CHAPTER 10

Preparing for the NFL Draft

B Y THE TIME the NFL draft rolled around in 1973, I had racked up a number of school and SEC records, which stood for a long time after I graduated, in other sports besides football. Back then there were no real constraints or NCAA rules that prevented an athlete from participating in more than one sport. Coach Bryant, however, did not want me working out with the wrestling or track teams. He was adamant that my full scholarship meant football was my priority and he was concerned I might get hurt and be unable to play football. While I couldn't work on drills and techniques with the wrestling and track teams, I was free to work on them in my off time.

Although I really didn't have enough free time to work out and improve my skills as best as I could, I had gotten so good at throwing the discus and hurling the shot put that the track coaches simply let me show up and compete in the meets most of the time. The strength training and conditioning I went through with the football program had prepared me well enough to be a serious competitor in these events, and when I left Alabama, I held the SEC record in both the shot put and discus.

When the 1972 Olympics in Munich were approaching, I gave very serious thought to trying out for the U.S. track team in shot put because I had recorded at least three throws where I came close to Wladyslaw Komar of Poland's gold medal-record of 69′6." If I had really worked at it, I'm sure I could have beaten that distance. I never really told anybody except Mom and Dad and maybe my brothers, but since professional football was my Holy Grail anyway and training for the Olympics would have made me miss the draft that year, I didn't make a serious effort to try and get on the team. But looking back on what could have been, I have some satisfaction, knowing that I could possibly have been the best shot put thrower in the world back then. It reminds me of the old fisherman in Ernest Hemingway's short story, *The Old Man and the Sea,* who caught the largest marlin in the world but didn't get to show it to anyone because the other predators in the sea ravaged it before he could row it back to shore.

I also wrestled my freshman year and had some matches my sophmore year. I won the SEC Heavyweight Championship my sophmore year. I wrestled some very big and tough guys to get there and I came close to making a mistake and almost let someone pin me a few times during the tournament. In those fleeting seconds when I believed he might be getting the upper hand at a critical point in the match, something deep inside me would ignite, and I would almost instinctively reach down and summon up an extraordinary strength to escape the hold. It was almost like I went blind with rage or fear that someone was going to control and embarrass me in front of my friends, teammates, coaches, and especially in front of my folks. That singular memory of getting my rear end whipped as a young boy and my dad chewing me out for not fighting back also provided some of the spark for tapping into that explosive strength every time I got in a potential jam on the mat.

When I later reviewed films of those matches, I realized in those moments of escape that I was doing something else I wasn't even aware of. When that flash of almost superhuman strength would surge, I roared so loudly I could be heard above the crowd watching the match. After the first time I heard that roar come from somewhere inside me, it startled me. I thought to myself, *What in the world was that?* It sounded inhuman like the rage of a trapped lion and, frankly, it scared me. I realized then that there was something terribly powerful buried inside of me that I couldn't control, an instinctive anger that exploded to rescue me from defeat. It was the ultimate internal defense system to make sure that no one—nothing—was ever going to hold me down and control me.

So when the 1973 NFL Draft was approaching, I had a fairly impressive resume in addition to my football record. I had earned eight letters in football, track, and wrestling. I held SEC records in the discus and shot put. I had been the SEC heavyweight wrestling champion, a two-time All-American football player, a member of the Crimson Tide All-Century team, and a member of the 1970s All-Decade Team.

I left Tuscaloosa and went home to Albertville, Alabama, to get some advice from Dad about what might happen in the draft. We sat out back on the terrace behind our home, and he talked with me as a full grown man and a trusted friend—not just as his son. Some of the same things he told me then would later be repeated during the introductory speech he gave for my induction into the Pro Football Hall of Fame. But hearing them for the first time and repeating them for you now brings tears to my eyes. "John, I want you to hear this from me, son. You have all the God-given talents that are the attributes of a great offensive guard," he said. "You're smart as can be. You're tough as nails, strong as a bull, and quick as a cat. You truly want to win and win fairly. Your attitude has been one of a true champion, and you're driven by an unusually strong ideal of attaining excellence. Plus you also have an unusually high tolerance for pain and have already shaken off injuries that would have knocked most every other player off the team."

This was the first time I had ever heard my dad give me an honest and thorough perspective of his approval and encouragement in such succinct and meaningful terms. My heart swelled as he spoke those words, and I remember thinking to myself, *I have really made my dad proud.* He continued: "John, you can be just as good as you want to be. I've known that since you were a little boy. The only thing standing between you and being the greatest lineman to ever live is *you*. I've told you all your life that you can't rest on your laurels, and if you always try to get better at what you do, with all the talents and gifts you were born with, one of these days the sportswriters just might say, 'That you were the best to ever play your position.' I also think you ought to get some recommendations about a good lawyer who might help with any contracts that might come your way during the draft. And if you do get drafted, you'll have to put your life on the line every single down to become the best you can be." When he finished those comments, my resolve was cemented that I was going to do whatever I had to in order to show my father that he was right. I was going to try and be the best lineman that ever played my position.

As I told you in the beginning, I am going to be brutally honest. So I have to tell you one thing about Coach Bryant I've really never told another human being. It's pretty widely known that when I got to the Patriots and began making enough of a name for myself as an offensive lineman, Coach Bryant was subsequently quoted as saying, "John Hannah is without a doubt the finest offensive lineman I've ever coached." In those years after I left Alabama and began playing for the Patriots, I found it really ironic and almost insulting that he said that—as if *he* was taking credit for my success and fame as a pro football player. Knowing back then what I'm about to tell you now, however, underscores my less-than-complete trust in Coach Bryant and my resentment toward how he sometimes treated me. I'm not trying to malign his image and reputation because he was a really great coach. I know many die-hard Alabama fans will be angry with me for telling this story, but I told you I was going to be honest.

After the talk with my dad, I thought I actually might have a chance to make it in the pros as did a few other people I respected. They told me I ought to hire a lawyer to help me through the process and to negotiate the best possible deal and suggested I talk to Coach Bryant. I intended to see Coach Bryant in his office after the Cotton Bowl against Texas to talk to him about names of lawyers who could help me during the upcoming NFL Draft. It wasn't necessarily an experience I looked forward to.

If you've ever seen pictures of his office—or been there—you know that the couch in front of his desk was set really low to the ground. You almost had to drop down into it. The height of the couch was part of a carefully planned strategy. Anyone sitting on the couch would be at a substantially lower spot in relation to his desk, and it was usually a player whose tail he was going to chew, an assistant he was going to fire, or someone he was going to suspend or kick off the team. It was a total power trip and intimidation thing—a control issue by implication and circumstance.

I had been in there once before at the end of my sophomore year. I had fallen in love with a girl, Page, who I really wanted to marry. I wanted to get married right then and not wait until after college. Any player, however, who wanted to get married, had to ask Coach Bryant for permission ahead of time.

I had to sit on that old battered sofa with the sawed off legs and stare up at him. My knees had ended up somewhere near my armpits. "Coach," I said, "I've met a girl I'm in love with and I want to marry her and well…I wanted to ask you if that was okay?" Bryant looked down at me from his high perch and said, "John, you know, some guys get married, and they go downhill quick. Others get married, and they do fine. I'm okay with it if you tell me you'll remain 100 percent committed to football."

Without hesitating I said, "Yes sir, I'll always be 100 percent committed to football first." In hindsight that's the way it remained throughout my first marriage—football always came first and the marriage second.

When I approached him this time, Bryant just spoke gruffly in that signature gravelly voice, "What do you want, John?" There was not a trace of pleasantry in his words. I cleared my throat, and said, "Well, Coach, you know….umm…the pro football draft is coming up, and well…I thought I might give it a try, and my dad said I might want to think about hiring a lawyer just in case, you know, to help me through it. I wondered if I could come talk to you after the Texas game and maybe get a recommendation from you?"

Coach Bryant didn't even look at me and said, "John, you ain't good enough to need a lawyer."

I just said, "Okay" and let him walk ahead of me.

As I walked back across the campus, I made a commitment to myself right then and there that I was going to show the world a thing or two about resolve and control. After all those hard seasons at Alabama where I gave him my very best effort and was instrumental in clutch plays on third-and-long in big SEC or bowl games when we badly needed yardage, perhaps one day I would prove Coach Bryant wrong. I opened the hole for Musso and the other backs so many times that I lost count.

The fact that Coach Bryant would dismiss and belittle me that way yet later proclaim to the world that I was "the finest offensive lineman he had ever coached!" burned my hair almost worse than my dad chewing me out so badly about letting that boy beat me up all those years earlier. But this time, I didn't get hurt...No, I got mad. I really resented Coach Bryant dismissing me so rudely—especially after I had given so much on the line to help the team and tried to make him look good as a coach in the process. The other accomplishments I had made in discus, shot put, and wrestling that put Alabama out front in those other areas, too, didn't seem to matter to him one bit. I was going to prove him wrong by showing that I was better than any lineman that he had ever seen or would ever see again. I was going to I strive to become the best offensive lineman to ever play the game.

I was selected as the fourth pick in the first round of the '73 draft by the New England Patriots.

CHAPTER 11

Becoming New England's Hog

I REMEMBER THE MIX of emotions I went through when the New England Patriots drafted me. One of the very first thoughts I had was how very wrong Coach Bryant had been in telling me I wasn't good enough to go pro. The pro scouts sure thought differently, however, and in 1973 I headed off to Boston, Massachusetts. I resisted the temptation to call Coach Bryant. I thought I might hear from him anyway with a small apology at writing me off so gruffly, but the call never came. In fact it would be many years later before I ever spoke another word with him. When he bragged to the world that I, John Hannah, was the finest offensive lineman he had ever coached, I always wondered if and how he remembered the truth about that curt exchange he had with me back in his office before the draft. I believe in my heart, however, he was really trying to motivate me because he knew how rough it was going to be in the pros.

Before moving to New England, I'd hardly been outside the state of Alabama in all of my 22 years except for some away games. And those trips were under strict conditions and rules with barely any free time to see much beyond the parking lots, locker rooms, and stadiums. So when I first went to Boston, just as my dad had described, it was like this young, country boy from Dixie was being whisked away to a strange city like Oz. I was excited but more than a bit scared and anxious. Overall, however, I was pretty cocky, being the second offensive lineman ever to be taken that high up in the draft. To the extent they could, my folks gave me some pretty good advice on many things, including how it might be easy for me to be taken advantage of by city slickers. Dad specifically reminded me to always trust God, stand my ground, and not let anyone push me around. As life in the pros began to unfold in Boston, I quickly forgot the first piece of that advice and started living almost totally in the realization that I was going to have to stand my ground and not let anybody push me around.

When I joined the Patriots in 1973, I had only very vague notions of what a decent salary and contract would entail. I was in Boston shortly after the draft for a banquet but didn't yet know what I was going to get paid. Coach Chuck Fairbanks took me and my wife, Page, off to the side and asked me to come into his office to talk about a contract. He started off by telling me that what he was about to offer me needed to stay very confidential (implying that other players might get mad if they ever found out how much he was going to pay me) and then he offered me a $20,000 bonus and a three-year contract with a starting salary of $25,000 and successive years of $27,000 and $30,000. I remembered that my dad's rookie contract with the New York Giants in 1951 was $6,000 and a $600 bonus, and the money Coach Fairbanks was offering me was a ton of money for someone from Albertville, Alabama. Still, I thought that a

Five-year-old Charley (*left*) stands next to his nine-year-old brother, John (*right*), in 1959.

From left to right, David (five), Charley (seven), and John (11) are dressed in their Sunday best for Easter of 1961.

The Hannahs treated their half-brother Ron (*seated*), who became the accountant for the Hannah family business, just like one of the boys.

The rough and tumble Hannah Boys at play as John (*left*) arm wrestles Charley (*right*). Herb, Coupe, and David look on in their Albertville, Alabama, home.

Charley (*left*) and John (*right*) pose together in April of 1986.

John Hannah endured a complicated relationship with legendary Alabama Coach Bear Bryant, who leans against a goal post in 1958. *(GETTY IMAGES)*

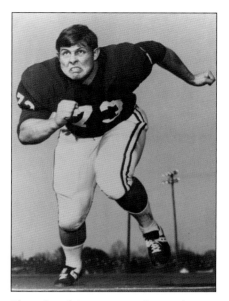

Showing his extreme intensity, John Hannah poses in 1971 during his Crimson Tide days. *(GETTY IMAGES)*

Displaying the impostor image that used to control him, John Hannah glares during a 1971 game in Tuscaloosa, Alabama. *(GETTY IMAGES)*

During Christmas of 1975 in Albertville, Alabama, John, Herb, and Charley (*back row, left to right*) and Major Luke Worsham, David, and Coach Bear Bryant (*front row, left to right*) commemorate David's signing with Alabama.

From left to right, John, Major Luke Worsham, David, and Charley celebrate during Christmas of 1975 as David becomes the third Hannah to sign with Alabama.

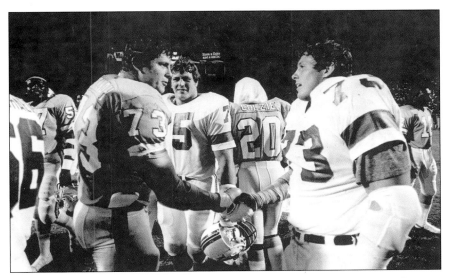

Charley Hannah (*left*) shakes hands with John Hannah (*right*) after a preseason contest between the Tampa Bay Buccaneers and the New England Patriots, representing one of the two games the brothers played against each other in the NFL.

John Hannah blocks Oakland Raiders linebacker Monte Johnson during the Raiders' 1976 divisional playoff victory, a game marked by questionable officiating. (*GETTY IMAGES*)

To craft the 1981 *Sports Illustrated* cover story, which declared John Hannah as "The Best Offensive Lineman of All Time," writer Paul Zimmerman spent a week with Hannah and his family in Albertville, Alabama. *(GETTY IMAGES)*

Wearing No. 73, the uniform number that carries so much meaning for him, John Hannah stands on the sideline during December of 1983. *(GETTY IMAGES)*

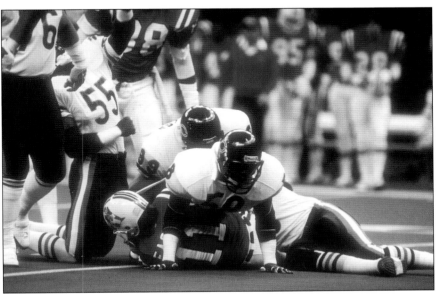

Patriots quarterback Tony Eason collapses under the pressure of the Chicago Bears defense during New England's 46–10 loss in Super Bowl XX, a crushing defeat, which represented the last game of John Hannah's career. *(GETTY IMAGES)*

John Hannah and his loved ones (*from left to right*)—Major Luke Worsham; John; son Seth; father Herb; and brother Charley—journey to John's Pro Football Hall of Fame induction in 1991.

From left to right, Andre Tippett, New England Patriots owner Bob Kraft, and John Hannah pose with Tippett's bust as the former Patriots linebacker is inducted into the Pro Football Hall of Fame in 2008. *(GETTY IMAGES)*

first-round draft pick ought to be worth more than what he was offering, so I told him I would have to think about it.

I hired an agent the next day. Mike Carroll was highly recommended to me, but when he only got the Patriots to move to $30,000, $35,000, $40,000, and $45,000 (with a $55,000 deferred bonus), I still thought that was low, but I didn't argue about it. Regardless, I was in the pros, making decent money for a young boy from Albertville and was ready to go to work. When the reality of this milestone in my career started to sink in, I was flooded with memories from my youth when we would go to church as a family and then rush home every week to watch the Sunday afternoon pro football games. Dad had infected all of us boys with a passion for professional football, and I was fascinated watching guys like Ray Nitschke, Gale Sayers, and Dick Butkus play their hardest as they absolutely mauled opponents like they owned the stadium.

Back then I often wondered if I would ever be good enough to play with those guys. After Red Miller served as my line coach for the Pats, his replacement was Jim Ringo, a two-time NFL champion as a Green Bay Packers offensive lineman. I once went up to Ringo and said, "Coach, do you think I could have played with those teams back in the '60s? Would I have been good enough?" Ringo looked me dead in the eye and said, "No question you could have played with them, John. None of them had all the gifts you have rolled up into one big package!"

Just after the draft concluded earlier that year, Sam Cunningham, the black running back from USC who was credited—rightly or wrongly—with doing more for integration in Alabama in 60 minutes than Martin Luther King Jr. did in 20 years during our embarrassing loss to USC in the opening game of the 1970 season, had been drafted by the Patriots, and we struck up a friendship right off the bat. The Patriots also selected Darryl Stingley, a wide receiver from Purdue. Those guys and I had been scheduled to be introduced as the first three Patriot picks in the draft, and the media asked us a whole bunch of questions. I will never forget one specific question I thought was both stupid and insulting. Someone asked me, "What it was going to be like to play on national television in front 55,000 fans?" I kind of chuckled real low because in my college career I had played in many televised games in front of 90,000 people at every home game and some away games in the SEC. I was a smart aleck, feeling my oats. I looked the reporter dead in the eye and said with as straight a face as I could, "Well, it won't be *too* disappointing."

1973 was a whirlwind. We had our first camp in Tampa, Florida, in early March because it was simply still too cold to practice effectively in Foxborough. After we finished down there, we headed back to camp in Foxborough for the months of April and May. Several of us in the rookie class were selected to play in the College All-Star Football Classic in Chicago, so we spent another two weeks up there preparing for that game in June. We also took a trip to the Pro Football Hall of Fame to watch the preseason Hall of Fame Game in Canton, Ohio, in mid-July.

There I got my first of many shocks about the realities of life in the pros. Some of the Patriots were playing in the game, and as Sam, Darryl, and I arrived, the hosts took us over to the stadium where the game had just gone into halftime. When we walked into the locker room, it was a massive fog of tobacco smoke. It seems like almost every player on the team had come in at halftime, and the first thing they did was light up a cigarette. I couldn't believe that was what pro football was like. These guys were in there smoking! Everything else was the same. They were getting water, washing off cuts and dirt, talking about specific plays, but they were sitting around smoking for crying out loud! I simply couldn't believe they were doing that kind of stuff. It was a real eye-opener for me to see the underbelly of a pro team like that for the first time. I would learn very quickly, however, that shock was going to be mild compared to what I would see later.

We arrived back in Boston and moved into our training camp at Amherst, Massachusetts, to work out even harder for the upcoming season. I know everybody talks about the luxuries of the NFL and the fancy clubhouses and team facilities, but I was surprised when I got the first inside look at the facilities of Foxborourgh Field in 1973, they were downright deplorable. The lockers were old and banged up, the sinks and toilets had long outlived their useful service, and everything else out of sight of the fans and media was downright crummy. The clubhouse was equipped with nothing state-of-the-art, and paint was peeling off walls just about everywhere you looked. There were only a couple of worn out massage tables, two old whirlpool spas, and little else. We were issued two uniforms and were responsible for washing them ourselves. If a jersey got torn or stained beyond respectability, we had to buy the replacements ourselves. The biggest surprise was that the rookies had to buy their own cleats.

■ | | | | ■

That College All-Star Football Classic in July of 1973 pitted the rookies, who had been college All-Stars, against the reigning Super Bowl champions, the Miami Dolphins. Even though the Dolphins won 14–3, that was a pretty big deal for me that first year. I met a bunch of the guys from other pro teams, including veterans who I had watched for years, and others who were rookies like me. Despite my private walk with God through those miserable penniless months working those cattle and struggling with my marriage, I was still very, very cocky when I got around other players. I thought I could hold my own with most of the bad boys, both on and off the field, and developed a serious penchant for messing with other players. It wasn't intended to be hurtful. It was just adults teasing and ribbing the other big boys, who most normal people would be afraid to look in eye—much less make fun of.

One of the best examples involves John Matuszak and Cullen Bryant. A bunch of us offensive linemen, who had played against those two behemoths, were at that All-Star Game in Chicago, and Matuszak and Bryant were there, too. Both of them were rookies like me, and both were big weightlifters who could bring a gym to a screeching halt as they put on a show by putting up ridiculous amounts of weight. They were amazingly strong—almost freakishly so—and it was hard to believe how big their muscles really were.

God bless him. Both of them were always wearing muscle T-shirts in the gym and out by the pool, making it a point to flex and act like they weren't posing as much as they possibly could, even though that's exactly what they were doing. They were real show-offs. So Pete Adams from Southern Cal and a couple of us others thought it would be funny if we took their game jerseys and cut the sleeves off to make them into sleeveless, muscle jerseys. We huddled up real quick, snipped their sleeves off, and threw them into the trash. After we hung the jerseys back in their lockers, we went off into the corner of the dressing room and acted like nothing had happened. But out of the corner of our eyes, we watched, laughing hysterically to ourselves.

These crazy, blown-up, muscle dudes came strolling in and saw their jerseys. And, to put it quite mildly, they didn't think it was funny at all. We had a hard time keeping our mouths shut to the other players and not taking credit for goofing on them so badly, but we didn't let on anything to anyone else. After all we were afraid they would beat the absolute living snot out of us. It was funny to us, but, Cullen and Matuszak, I apologize to you posthumously, old boys.

■ | | | | ■

As for learning the game of pro football, it was a lot different than anything I could have expected. In pro camp in Tampa, Florida, I met Coach Miller, my offensive line coach. That's when I realized I was in a whole new game. Everything was so different about the philosophy and process of pro ball with the Patriots. It was like I was just starting to learn how to play football all over again. Coach Miller insisted the linemen set up in a three-point stance, something I had never done. It felt awkward and nothing like I had been used to for years on the line. The linemen also had to learn pass protection by pulling off, backing up, and standing ground as the defense came rushing in. This form of "retreat" pass protection was totally foreign to me as I was so used to blowing off the line as hard as I could and taking the game to the defense instead of dropping back and waiting for them to come barreling in.

It totally went against my mind-set and gut instincts and, quite frankly, it was really hard for me. That kind of soft offensive posture robbed me of one of the most positive assets that had gotten me to the pros to begin with: my ability to run into the oncoming defense and get the jump on them. Instead I had to wait for them to get a full head of steam as they charged in while they hit me as hard as they could.

I had never been a pulling guard before because everything we had done so successfully at Alabama with the wishbone was straight up and straight ahead. It suddenly became a very tough time for me as I struggled to undo many years of playing habits and offensive line moves I was comfortable with. At camp they were working me like a plow mule every day. I would get through with practice, and even though the other guys left to go shower and change, Coach Chuck Fairbanks or Coach Miller would make me hang back and continue to work me some more after practice, hoping that would bring me along quickly. I guess in some ways that was a compliment or at least I took it that way. Regardless, I worked my derriere off and I was exhausted at the end of each day like I had never been before. I had never once foreseen being in a situation as grueling as that rookie training turned out to be. Additionally, even though I wasn't necessarily tall or super heavy by any pro standard, the combination of the hot air and the brutal extra training caused me to lose a lot of weight I really couldn't afford to lose. I had always had a problem with being too heavy, but with the extreme regimen I was on and the extra work to boot, I was fighting to keep my weight up.

I was working so hard I almost killed myself. I was also tired back home of my wife, who could have cared less what kind of grueling work I was doing, and she was constantly complaining about this and that and everything totally irrelevant to what I was trying to accomplish. A few times I told her this on the phone and simply hung up on her. My attitude with her soured and so did my personality. So at the end of March 1973 when I finally got back to Boston, I guess everything finally caught up with me. To only my mild shock, all the furniture, pictures, dishes, and everything else Page and I had bought for our house had been packed up, and she was gone.

That was the part of the pro football world that I wasn't prepared to handle: balancing home life and a marriage against the high life of living like a gladiator. That was the first time we ever split up, and I recognize now a lot of it was my fault—not all of it—but certainly the major share. Eventually she came back, and we tried to work it out for a long, long time. But the pain and hard feelings from that first separation never quite healed, and eventually we divorced in 1996.

■ | | | | ■

Miller nicknamed me "Hog" early on in my rookie season with the Patriots. We were in the film room watching plays from a scrimmage where we had driven the ball down to the 1-yard line. I disobeyed the order to use the three-point stance and reverted to my old four-point stance in the next play. But Coach Miller yelled out, "Way to root hog him out of there," and immediately, Bill Lenkaitis, the starting center we called "Lenk," started hollering "Hog, Hog, Hog," and from then on, I was known as "Hog" Hannah.

Right after the Anhorst camp had finished, I think my weight had dropped from about 280 down to 255, even though I was eating and drinking everything in sight, trying to keep my weight on. Coach Miller had wanted me to stay around 275, and it was horrible trying to keep up. I had to stuff myself with high-calorie meals and drink water, sports drinks, sodas, and whatever else by the gallon.

While we were in camp, I learned that amphetamines were commonly used by more than a couple of players. Poppers, dex (dexamphetamine), speed, lightning, uppers were just a few of the nicknames for the pills many players would take before a game. I also learned pretty quickly that cocaine was not off limits either. When some of that became public, any player who was found to be using illegal drugs or substances, he supposedly would be dismissed from the team. In my judgment that order was purely for public consumption. And to my knowledge, even though the use of amphetamines continued unabated, no Patriots player was ever disciplined—much less dismissed from the team—because we continued to win. If the public might have been offended by hearing some players used speed, well, those rumors stopped.

Late in my career just before Super Bowl XX with the Chicago Bears, some nosy reporter with *The Boston Globe* got wind of several players using amphetamines and was going to do a story on the subject right after the Super Bowl. I've always felt that we played so poorly in that game because so many guys were distracted with worry about what the story might say and who would be implicated.

As I started to learn more about the other players, it also became very clear some of the guys were just nutty paranoids who were slaves to all sorts of phobias or rituals. They had weird patterns or superstitious routines they would follow to psyche themselves up for games. More than a few of them rocked back and forth on the locker room bench and muttered incoherently to themselves while others paced incessantly, slammed all the open locker doors, bloodied their fists by repeatedly hitting cinder walls, and yelled a stream of horrific obscenities at themselves in the bathroom mirror. A lot of stuff got broken in the locker room before every single game.

Then there was another segment of players who were just regular guys, experiencing the pregame jitters just like any other high school or college player would. Some prayed, some vomited a couple of times, or a few might have cried. Others just sat very still, hands clenched and looking at the floor, squinting their eyes shut as they mentally prepared themselves for the combat about to unfold. I can't say exactly what group I belonged to, but I was probably a member of all those clubs at one point during my 13 years with the Patriots.

CHAPTER 12

From Intimidated Rookie to Intimidating Veteran

s I GOT more comfortable living so far north of Dixie, I began to realize what an incredible and fascinating city Boston is. The richness of its history lives on practically every corner. It has a very cool feel, and the city has largely been able to stay on the cutting edge of current advances in almost everything while still holding very fast and firm to its historical roots that are among the deepest in our country. Much of the architecture of homes and buildings still has a colonial feel to it while the financial district and business center of the city are tastefully modern and current. Historical charm just oozes out of just about everything in Boston.

The more I learned about Boston and its interesting population, I also realized how fervent the New England Patriots fans were and what a huge following the Patriots had nationwide. I quickly learned the names of many business tycoons and old-line, blue-blood families that had poured massive amounts of money into the Patriots' programs. The media and television sponsors were regularly paying obscene amounts of money to advertise their names in association with the team. Billy Sullivan, the owner of the franchise at the time I was drafted, was a native Bostonian businessman who had bought the rights to the American Football League's eighth and final franchise for $25,000 in 1959. His sons, Patrick and Chuck, held executive positions with the team, and by 1964 Billy Sullivan had struck a deal with NBC television to broadcast AFL games.

Two years before I signed, the name of the team had been changed from the Boston Patriots to the New England Patriots as the franchise moved its home field to Schaefer Stadium in Foxborough, Massachusetts. The list of shareholders and corporate partners of the Patriots was just incredible, and the roster of celebrities from every conceivable field—movie stars, pro basketball players, golfers, artists, singers, performers, race car drivers—many of whom held box seats and season tickets, was nothing short of stunning.

Although I would in fact meet many of those people later in my career, it was a huge shock to discover that they wanted to meet *me* more than I wanted to meet them. Even as arrogant as I was becoming, the idea that I was a star player who celebrities would come to admire and love was nowhere in my universe of thought that first season. The vast majority of the Boston population is just great, and as my playing stature with the Patriots began to grow, I was embraced by what seemed like a majority of the fans.

Another first about my rookie year with the Patriots was that it was the first year in my entire life I experienced some true freedom. It's like I had made it through the boot camp of life, spending those three long, miserable years at Baylor and having successfully run the gauntlet of playing for Coach Bryant. Now I was finally on my own two feet. I had married Page, a pretty, little girl from back home in Alabama, and Boston was indeed like Oz for a big ol' redneck like me. After getting selected fourth overall and receiving a decent salary for a farm boy from Alabama, I started getting a big head about being the first lineman to ever go that high up in the pro draft.

My head actually swelled *really* big, and I began to argue with my wife. I was the big-shot boss now and started going out at night with some buddies, and she was *not* going to tell me what I could and couldn't do. I went out night after night and started having a pretty good time for myself, often drinking the night away. Eating and drinking whatever I wanted to was something I had never experienced, and more and more nights, I left Page at home. I often returned in the early morning hours drunker than I realized.

With this new sense of freedom and no one telling me what to do, where to go, and when to be there, I went a little crazy. I started to live life somewhat to excess. I'd go out with even more of my new teammates and drink way too much. I'd gorge myself on all sorts of different foods that Boston was famous for. I even bought some new hip clothes befitting of a rising pro player. I was working very hard to become part of the accepted crowd of big shots, and the fans in Boston simply loved seeing their Patriots out in public. I loved the attention they showered on me when they would spot me and a bunch of the other guys out eating and drinking. The early recognition and attention that year was unlike anything I had ever experienced, and I wanted as much of it as I could get.

After we settled into training camp back home, we were housed in a dormitory that was hot as Hades that time of the year. Believe it or not, July can be brutally hot in Boston. The beds in the dorm were awful, too, and most everybody took the frame of their bed, threw it to the side of the room, and put their mattress on the floor, which at least gave the big guys a little more support than those sagging old bed frames did. There was no air conditioning in the entire place, so everybody had fans going. They helped some, but I mean it was just downright miserable. Even though I was from the Deep South and ought to have been used to the heat, all the hard work of training became coupled with the lack of sleep from the horrible beds and hot night air, and the situation we were in was simply awful.

The anticipation of the first game was really unbelievable, but I more distinctly remember my third preseason game. As we rode out to the stadium in buses to play the New York Giants, I was shocked to see a whole lot more Giants fans at the game than Patriots fans. I got to start in that game, and Rich Glover, a rookie defensive lineman from Nebraska who had been drafted by the Giants, played in front of me more than anybody else. And with both of us being rookies, we had a pretty good matchup, and I think we both enjoyed our first game a lot more than if we had been banging it out against some old veterans who would pull out all the tricks to welcome us to the league. What I remember most of all about that game was the satisfaction of getting the first one under my belt and not making a total fool of myself in the process.

I started the first 13 games of my rookie season. I quickly dispelled some lingering concerns by the quarterback and running back coaches that I might have a hard time adjusting from the straight-ahead blocking style used in the wishbone offense to the drop-back and pulling program required of the offensive guards in the pros. Coach Jim Ringo noticed something he thought was pretty unusual in how I used my feet and introduced me to the idea that I could enhance my abilities even more by adopting a cross-step technique of lateral movement. By being able to switch one foot over the other, as opposed to shuffling my feet side by side, I was able to move side to side even more quickly. And in the NFL, success is often measured in half seconds. I mastered the cross-step technique in little time, and my lateral speed in pass blocking or pulling to lead for Steve Grogan or a running back became one of my trademarks. Due to their larger size and bulk, not many other offensive linemen ever truly mastered that technique, but just as Major Worsham had gotten me to practice running the straight lines to get rid of my duck walk, I practiced the cross step repeatedly until I got it down pat and used it for all it was worth.

We then got into the opening games of my rookie season, and I can't describe what it was like for me to play in my first professional football contests. One of the earliest games we played was against the Kansas City Chiefs. I played in front of a huge guy named Buck Buchanan, who played defensive right tackle. Buck was from a small town outside of Birmingham, Alabama, called Gainesville. Buck had played college ball at Grambling State, a historically all-black school, and was a seasoned vet in the ranks of pro football. When I got down in the stance and looked across at him, I swear, he was the biggest man I had ever seen. He was about 6'7" and probably weighed 300 pounds. He looked at me and said "Homeboy, I'm going to teach you to play in the NFL today." I said to myself, *Oh, Lord, here we go.*

We started playing, and I remember when the first pass situation was called, and our quarterback, Jim Plunkett, was setting up in the pocket. I got up in my pass stance but raised up way too high. I guess I lost my focus for a moment, but that big old player across the line took full advantage of my temporary mental lapse. Buchanan grabbed me under the armpits and lifted me straight off the ground. It was horrifying to feel my toes dragging the ground and him standing there lifting me up, and I swear he actually walked me backward toward Plunkett as he basically manhandled me. All the time Buchanan was giggling, "hee, hee!" When he got to Plunkett, he threw me aside and then he just killed Jim. He also killed me that whole day.

When I got inducted into the Pro Football Hall of Fame in 1991, all the other living members of the Hall were on the stage behind me, and as my dad was introducing me, I heard Buck in the background talking to somebody. Buchanan said, "Did you ever play in front of that Hannah kid?" I think he was speaking to Dick Butkus, who replied, "Yeah, yeah, I played against him when he was real young."

"Yeah, me too," Buchanan said. "He sho' musta gotten a *whole* lot better since then to get here." And I heard both of them chuckle real hard. Being among all those other pro football greats was always a humbling experience.

We also played against Butkus and the Chicago Bears that year. Butkus was 6'3" and 245 pounds of solid muscle and was one of the most intimidating linebackers in all of professional football. *Sports Illustrated* put him on the cover in 1970 under the heading: "The Most Feared Man in the Game." Many players regarded him as just plain mean and nasty. The Patriots had a little running back named Mack Herron, who was about 5'6" and weighed about 170 pounds. We called him "Mini Mack" because he was so small for an NFL player, but he was a real good running back. He was a fireplug, but he had a tendency to be real mouthy and sassy and he was calling Butkus every name in the book. Right off the bat, I knew that was not a smart thing to do at all.

We had this play we called P12, where our center, Bill Lenkaitis, would take on the middle linebacker, and I would block the defensive tackle. But because Butkus was so hard to contain, the center, who had the nicknames of "Lenk," "the Missing Link," and "Bucket Head," would shift and call a fold. During a fold, Lenk would come firing out on the tackle, and I would come out of the chute and take on the middle linebacker.

Every time we ran that P12 play, which we did a lot, Lenk would call a fold. After about 20 times running that play, Butkus finally figured out what fold meant.

And then every time a fold was called, that tank of a linebacker would run right up the chute, hit me like a freight train, and knock the snot out of me. I finally asked Lenk to give me some false calls or something because Butkus was murdering me, but Lenk wouldn't do it. Finally, late into the third quarter, I told him, "You haven't given me any false calls…The next time you call fold, and I know I can't block him, I'm going to call it off." We lined up for the next play. Mini Mack is calling Butkus a whole bunch of nasty names, and all of a sudden, Lenk yells out for a fold and I say, "No." He calls for a fold again, and again I say, "No!" The ball is snapped, and both Lenk and I block the tackle, and nobody even touched Butkus. He blew by us like a mad bull and knocked Herron into next week. Needless to say, Mini Mack never said anything else the rest of the day. I think that hit from Butkus was enough payback that it took Herron's voice away for good.

Another funny memory I have of my rookie year is when we ran a play where I pulled to the right. It was the first time we had called that play, and when I pulled, I suddenly noticed the defensive backs were running in the other direction. As a pulling guard, I figured the ball carrier must have changed at the last moment or there was a lateral or something, so I instantly reversed, turned around, and started running to the other side. To my absolute amazement, the defensive backs suddenly turned around also and started running back the other way. Not knowing what was happening, I turned around again and chased them back the other way. This happened three or four times, and I still couldn't figure out what was going on. Each pulling play like that, we lost about five yards. While we were pinned back on the 15 or maybe 10-yard line, the defensive backs suddenly just stopped in their tracks. A couple of them had the most bewildered look on their face I had ever seen in a game.

I turned around and saw our running back, John Tarver, with the ball in his hands. He bent over, put it between his legs, and then threw the football backward all the way over the top of his head and out of the end zone and into the stands. The official ruled it a safety, and by rule our opponent received the next possession. As I was sitting on the sidelines and waiting for the offense to go back in, I was sitting next to Tarver and was very curious why he decided to do that. "What in the world was that? I've never seen anything like that," I said. "What made you do that?"

"Well, John, I thought if I threw it out of bounds or over the end zone like that, it would be a touchback, and we would not have to punt," Tarver said. "That way we wouldn't continue to lose so much yardage with you running the wrong way." That was the way pro football was with the Patriots that first year. I was constantly learning new moves and tricks and also learning some serious lessons in humility, too.

Just before the last game of that first season, we were practicing punt protection, and the linemen would lay out or back pedal to assist the backs in protecting the punter from a defensive rush or outright blitz. When I laid out, a rushing defensive lineman came through and caught me totally by surprise. He hit me precisely the wrong way and broke my left leg. It was a complete freak accident, so even though I had started all 13 games of my rookie season, I had to miss the last game. As banged up as I was, I can't say I was completely disappointed to get to sit one out—even if it was the final game.

I went back home to Alabama with a cast on my leg, and the Patriots' season ended with a miserable 5–9 record. Dad asked me if I wanted to go to a function with him. There was a real estate agent we knew very well in Albertville named Fred Taylor, who hosted a huge Christmas party every year. It would be a great time to catch up with a lot of my hometown friends, find out what had been going on back home, and share some of my experiences about what life in professional football was like.

After the draft and before I left for Boston earlier that year, I found out that another guy in Albertville was laying bets that pro ball would be too much for me to handle and I would quit or get cut from the Patriots and be back home after one season. I had heard he made a lot of bets with different people on his negative prediction that I would wash out after one season. Well, when I heard about those bets before I took off for Boston, it made me mad as all get out, but it also motivated me even more to stick it out, make the team, and play the best I could. I wanted to be proud of myself. I wanted my family, friends, Coach Bryant, my hometown of Albertville, and the state of Alabama to be proud of me.

So I went to Taylor's Christmas party with Dad, and, sure enough, that guy showed up and walked around. When I first saw him, I got more than a little upset and became downright mad. I was sure some of the people—who believed I would make it in the pros, took those bets with him, and took his money in the process—were at the party, too. I made up my mind right there that I was going to embarrass him in front of as many people as I could. After saying hello I said I was very sorry to hear about all the money he had lost that year. He said, "Well, John, it has been a really tough year, you know? The farm industry hasn't been nearly as good as I thought it was going to be, and I have way too much inventory and equipment left that I haven't been able to sell."

"No, no, no, not *that* money," I said. "I'm sorry you lost all those bets you made on me not making it in the pros my first season." I gave him a big smile as I walked off. By the look on his face, it was clear as a bell that he was shocked and grossly embarrassed to realize that I knew about the losing bets he had made against me. It was a great feeling for me to gloat a little and lord it over him that way. It was also in some, strange way a vindication or validation of some sort that oddly reassured me of my ability to make it on my own in the tough world of professional football and to put to rest any lingering doubts by anyone that I could stand my ground. That rookie season, however, had been a really, really long year, and I got my butt handed to me in just about every game.

If it hadn't been for coach Red Miller constantly encouraging me, I probably *would* have thought about giving up because it was just a disastrous, depressing start to my professional career. But seeing the embarrassment on that guy's face who bet against me just underscored my earlier resolve that I was not going to leave after only one season. I had too much pride in myself. I certainly did not want to disappoint my family nor did I want to give Coach Bryant any reason to think he was actually right in the "advice" he gave me about turning pro.

My smug satisfaction over that guy losing those bets faded pretty quickly because God was about to give me a small wake-up call to remember where He fit in the whole scenario. Another major mistake I made that first season was to not properly plan and account for how my pay from the Patriots would be budgeted over an entire year. We got 14 game checks back then, and since I was the No. 4 draft pick, I signed a negotiated contract for an aggregate $200,000 for four years. They gave me a $55,000 deferred signing bonus, and the total salary would be paid out at $30,000 the first year, $35,000 the second, $40,000 the third, and $45,000 the fourth year. Aside from the bonus, my first year's salary would be paid in 14 installments as the games were played throughout the season, and it would be paid out the same way during the next three years at the annually increased salaries.

When I got my hands on that first game check, I didn't think that each of those game checks was all I was going to get for the whole year. I needed to monitor how it was spent and to put some away for savings to live on the rest of the year. My wife, Page, had come back to me after she left me while I was in camp in Tampa, and we were both spending money left and right. All of a sudden, we realized we were almost completely out of money. Although Page had fully accepted Christ into her life years before and lived in submission to his power and will, she and I were still trying to get used to one another and were not doing a very good job. Things started to look very bleak when we realized we had spent ourselves almost broke.

However, I did obtain one very valuable asset from Coach Fairbanks himself. Right before the season ended, he asked me, "What do you want to accomplish in pro football, John?" After I said I wanted to reach a Super Bowl, he replied, "That's what we all want John...What do you want, John? I mean you as an individual?" I told him without hesitating: "I want to be the best offensive lineman that ever played the game." After he asked me what it would take to make that happen, I acknowledged that the first thing would have to be a coach who could teach me, really teach me, and get me where I wanted to be.

Coach Fairbanks told me to see him if I ever had an issue that stood in the way of attaining that goal to become the best lineman ever. So at the end of the 1977 season, I went to him with an issue. I told him I didn't think I could accomplish my goal of becoming the best offensive lineman to ever to play the game with the coach I had and that the offensive line coach had to be replaced. When we reported back for summer camp for the

1978 season, we had a new offensive line coach, Jim Ringo. He is the absolutely best offensive coach that I ever had and he taught me more about how to play football than any man I've ever met in my life.

After the season ended, Page and I went back home to Albertville, and since we were so hurting for money, Dad gave me a job. He wanted me to work the Hannah Supply store he had opened in Montgomery, so I could learn the business in south Alabama. There, however, wasn't quite enough work going on there to support us, so I took an additional job with the Allen Taylor Cattle Company right outside Montgomery, helping move the cattle through the yard and chutes, giving them antibiotic shots, neutering them, and cutting their horns so they'd become steers. It was nasty, miserable work in the scorching Alabama heat. I felt pretty bad, coming off my rookie season as the fourth over-all pick in the NFL draft who still had to work like this during the summer just to survive because I hadn't done a good enough job watching my money. Page didn't make it any easier on me either.

One brutally hot afternoon, I was sitting alone in the restroom, contemplating the mess we were in and trying to figure out what to do, when I suddenly thought about the guy I had roomed with that rookie year, Allen Gallaher. He had been drafted from Southern Cal and was a very strong, very confident Christian who privately and quietly shared his witness with me the entire year. Nothing seemed to faze Gallaher, and I was somewhat amazed at the quiet strength he was able to summon and rely on through his faith alone. Finally I started praying in earnest, something I hadn't done in quite a while. I said, "Lord? I know you are here, God. Please God, please help me out here. I'm in trouble and I don't know what to do and I'm afraid God."

I became very quiet and closed my eyes and I began hearing his words of comfort come to me. He asked me to let Him back into my heart and soul and to let Him show me the way through this financial mess and rocky relationship with the woman I had married. And that night I read all four gospels back to back, trying to figure out what his word meant for me and how I could invite Him fully into my life. I found myself accepting Christ again and once more I asked Him to be fully in me. Even though I had accepted Him many years before, the difference was that I experienced the sweetness of his love and rightful place in my life and then moved on under my own will. This time, however, I accepted Christ and honestly tried to be pleasing to Him under his will. Somehow, Page and I got through it. We became more comfortable and respectful of each other, and the change in our relationship and circumstances was unbelievable. We made it through that year by working and praying together, and things really did get better. For the first time in my life, I found that I really wanted to please God and I was working very hard to do so. Things continued to get much better, and that's when we decided to buy a little house in Albertville.

■ | | | | ■

The freak leg injury that forced me out of the final game of my rookie season was the first of many I would sustain while I stayed in the game of professional football, and surgery became almost as commonplace as shaving. It seems like every time I turned around, I was getting something cut or repaired. Many times I had multiple surgeries on the same area. My shoulders and knees took on more scars than a carnival bumper car, and I lost count of how many broken fingers and bones I endured. As I write this, I'm probably three years or more overdue for a total left knee replacement, and every step I take up and down the stairs is a constant, screaming reminder of the thousands of downs I played.

I took a trip, my dad had won, to Italy late that summer of 1974 and spent a long time thinking about how I got to where I was, how my dad had supported and encouraged me when I was broke, and how Christ helped me pull through working in Montgomery and reconciling with Page. I also began recalling how many other times *both* Dad and Christ had carried me through so many other low points in my life and led me to some unusually good things as well. I was sitting quietly in one of the ancient cathedrals and I suddenly realized that I wanted—no needed—to show my dad how very much I appreciated all his help through the years to get me where I was.

Through Coach Fairbanks, I asked the Patriots to renegotiate my contract. He went to bat for me and teammate Leon Gray, too, with Billy Sullivan, the team owner. He reported back that they would extend my contract for *another* three years with a deferred bonus through 1979 and modest annual increases with an option for one more year through 1980. Coach Fairbanks acknowledged the figures they were talking about weren't "top dollar" but promised me that my salary would be reviewed every year and upgraded if I ranked "with the top linemen in the league." Unfortunately, that never happened. It certainly wasn't Coach Fairbanks' fault as all the money decisions were made by Billy Sullivan and his sons, Chuck and Pat.

With the negotiated deferred bonus and additional bonus I got for extending my contract another three years totaling $55,000 was announced, it was touted as the largest bonus ever paid to a lineman in the pros. My first instinct was to offer it to my dad for him to invest in the continued growth of Hannah Supply and its related businesses. It made me feel very mature and level-headed. To my surprise, however, he politely turned me down, which caught me totally off guard. I had offered it to him as my way of a son thanking his dad for all the encouragement and support he had shown me through the years. I thought it was a gesture of honor and the fulfillment of a noble family duty. He didn't even consider taking it, and simply told me, "No thanks, John, I don't need it. If you want to do something more meaningful with it than investing in a farm supply company, I'm sure something will come to you."

I decided to call my old teammate, John Croyle. John and I had been friends at Alabama and had gotten to know each other fairly well. He came up to Albertville that summer of 1974 and talked to me about a vision he had of opening a ranch for unfortunate children. It was his calling. I knew he had come up under hard circumstances and didn't have some of the extra things my folks had been able to give me, but he had an incredibly strong faith that replaced everything he lacked in the trappings of the world. In all the years I had known him, he never bad-mouthed his upbringing at all. He was one of the teammates who was never shy about talking about his faith and praying in public before a meal.

When he drove up to my house and as he got out of his truck, I was reminded how tall and rangy he was. He was strong as an ox, stood nearly 6'7", and had a tough country swagger that spoke loudly that he was not someone to mess with despite the soft spot in his heart. I always thought Croyle was one of the toughest defensive ends I had ever seen and I had suggested that he might consider the professional draft at the same time I did. He laughed me off with a resolute no. He simply said, "I've got something better to do, John, and I'm going to figure out a way to make this safe ranch thing happen for these kids."

"What are you talking about, John? You're in the pros, boy," he said. "You got places to go, people to see, and trophies to win."

"I'm not talking about working with you, John. I just want to help you start the kid's ranch," I said. "I got an advance on the deferred bonus the Patriots gave me and I want to do something to honor God with it, but I got to ask you a favor first. If I give you this money, will you promise me you'll never tell anybody where it came from?"

He looked at me and blinked a couple of times and said: "What are you saying, John? You want to lend me the advance on your bonus?" I replied, "No, John, I want to *give* it to you—$30,000 of it. It's just that I don't want you to tell anybody that I gave it to you. One of the lessons my folks taught me is that when you give something to the glory of God, you keep it only between Him and you. Can you promise me you won't tell anybody where the money came from?"

Well, God bless him, he did promise me that, and I gave him the $30,000 advance from the bonus. The first thing he did, however, was tell everybody that John Hannah had given him most of his signing bonus to start what would become known as Big Oak Ranch. My first instinct was to be chapped at him for violating a trust and breaking his promise, but I soon guessed that when he suddenly began spending this money and buying land and lumber for a dormitory, some folks might have gotten suspicious and begun wondering where the money came from. I really did want my gift to remain anonymous because I also didn't want people thinking I had bought good will by announcing I was helping establish the home for underprivileged children. I just wanted to keep it between Him and me and God. But I know now more and more, the good Lord has *always* been in control. Since I couldn't control John's enthusiasm or anxiety at keeping the source of funds secret, it's not mine to second guess or condemn him, and I forgave John for breaking his vow of silence many moons ago.

■ | | | | ■

The 1974 season rolled around and I was re-energized and ready to be starting up front again. After my rookie season, I had become a known quantity as a lineman for the Patriots, and all the opposing teams' defensive coaches started coming up with new plays and strategies to run against me whenever they played the Patriots. Even with a year under my belt, my football was still not as good as it needed to be. I was not playing like I needed to play. We started out the year and had a few big successes, but at the end of the year, due to injuries and stuff like that, we ended up at .500.

When we played the Cowboys one game, Richard Cole, my high school coach from Albertville, came to visit me. Lee Roy Jordan was playing linebacker for the Cowboys. Jordan was from Alabama and had always been my hero, a guy I looked up to and someone who had also played for Coach Bryant. When we got into the game, we got into the run formation and Lenk called fold, I pulled up, went through the chute, and I hit Jordan, but he stopped me like a brick wall. Another player immediately fell on the back of my legs, and Jordan pushed me back, bent me over, and said, "Golly bum, Hannah. Coach Bryant would be so embarrassed by you." That really made me mad, but more than anything it was terribly embarrassing.

Jordan got in my head that game, and I played terribly the rest of the contest. I think I gave up about five sacks to him in that game. What made it even worse was how awful I played in front of my old high school coach and a few friends who had come to the game with him. After that game and into the rest of the season, I was really trying to get better, but I still wasn't improving very much. But daylight finally dawned on Marblehead, (Massachusetts)—as they say in New England—

when we played the Oakland Raiders. I lined up in front Otis Sistrunk, who was just huge at 6'5" and 265 pounds, strong as Goliath, and tough as a knotty oak.

When I first got down in my stance across from him, his forearm was so massive it looked like he had three legs. Otis intimidated me, and I played scared the whole game just like I had the previous year and a half. Oakland beat us badly, and I think I also let several sacks go down on my watch. After the game I got on the bus and went straight to the back. I didn't want to talk to anybody. I sat there brooding and fuming, thinking about everything I had done wrong. All of a sudden, it struck me. I thought, *Why are you so scared, Hannah? You're not hurt. You're not beat up. What's wrong with you? Why don't you just gut up and start doing this?* In those next few moments, things suddenly began to gel, and that was the real turning point in my pro career.

I realized right then that instead of continuing to worship the guys I always dreamed about playing in front of, I needed to play without fear. I thought, *Hey! I am here playing with these guys and I'm good enough to play against them. I am that guy who's fighting against them now and I don't need to be scared. I can compete against them and I'm not going to let them intimidate me anymore.*

That whole shift in my perspective and attitude really opened things up and took me a significant step forward in my career. My play started to improve immediately. We were all on the same field, and it was mostly level, and I was going to learn better techniques without being intimidated. I made a conscious decision to give it all I had, try to get better every game, and to play with a whole lot more confidence.

As my confidence firmed up and my performance improved, so did my Christian faith. People began to notice a big difference in me. I wasn't going out anymore and doing the things I had when I went a little crazy with the freedom I experienced my rookie year. I was more open and vocal about my faith, and while everybody knew that I was a Christian, the problem was my faith still wasn't fully mature or as deeply rooted as God wanted. I wasn't resting in Him. My faith in Jesus at that time, and for the next several years, was primarily about God blessing me. I wasn't seeking to please God and do his will because I primarily wanted my will to be his will. I wanted Him to bless what I wanted to do, to bless my actions, and bless my games, so that I could play better and bless my life so that I could earn a lot of money. I would decide what I wanted to do and ask for God's blessing instead of the other way around.

It was a very, very selfish faith. In a way I felt if I could please God by being obedient to Him, I would be entitled to receive those blessings. At the same time, I also began to get lost in a lot of the legalism in the bible that began to creep into my life. In some ways, I became hypocritical in my private life as contrasted with the outer face of Christian piety I adopted. I also became condescending and judgmental about others and began to hold a holier than thou, sanctimonious attitude, and I know now God was not pleased.

In a couple of games that season, I got hit with some pretty cheap shots. Back then NFL referees let more go. I don't really know why. Maybe it was the strict time limits we had on television slots, and neither team wanted a game unnecessarily prolonged because of a bunch of excessive penalties. Maybe it was just the gladiator syndrome of humans who expected that professional players ought to be more violent and hit harder because that was a big part of what the fans paid good money to come and watch.

In the process of psyching myself up to do battle game after game, I also gradually lost sight of the amazing reassurance of putting God first in all things. The memories were still there, but the heat of the moments in professional football slowly pushed Him to the bench instead of keeping Him right there with me on the line. But football back then was all about high-speed collisions, and the faster I ran and harder I played, the less time I dwelled on keeping communion with Him. No matter how banged up I was from earlier collisions, I'd go into a zone before games where I would visualize myself hitting an opponent. I mean *really* hitting him—as hard and often as I could. I would make myself see hitting the other guy and succeeding. I could stir up awful amounts of intense anger and resentment and would drive myself to the point of really wanting to *hurt* my opponent. I'd get in that zone—I used to call it "nutso-frenzy"—a mind-set of almost higher consciousness where everything else was totally blocked out except hitting a guy across the line so hard I'd believe I heard bones snapping.

Another Patriot, Brian Holloway, who used to play tackle next to me, once described me as a "turbine in a nuclear plant" because he knew how intense I was and how much I hated losing. But he and the other players also knew to stay away from me on gameday. No one had better try to talk to me then as it would break my concentration, and I'd fly into a rage at them. And facing "Hog" Hannah when he was in a rage back then would have been a very serious mistake. My being so tightly wound on gameday became so well known—and I guess feared—in the Patriots locker room that I was the only player who got my own dressing area away from the other guys. The only guy who would ever willingly have a locker next to me was a black guy from Miami, Ronnie Lippett, and that was only because he had nearly the same kind of focus I did. People knew to stay out of his way, too. Looking back on it now, I can't believe that my biggest fear—looking like a jerk and losing—became the very source of my looking like a jerk and I lost a lot of good relationships in the process.

When it comes right down to it, I got a huge, sick rush off hitting and hurting other guys. I would go tunnel vision-blind, zero in on an enemy jersey, and run into it with all the speed and force I could play after play. I knew that when I heard a certain primal, guttural noise come out of an opposing player, I had popped him with a lick like he had never taken before. And I would think to myself, *By gosh, he'll remember and respect me the next time we meet!* I especially enjoyed delivering that first crushing blow to those new guys across the line or the ones back in the secondary. I developed an almost sinister pleasure in hitting them harder and making them hurt more than they could have ever imagined, especially the cocky punks who had talked trash to me before we actually got down to business. More than a few times, I hit those guys so hard that they either laid down on the field for a while or left on a stretcher. Maybe a couple or more of them left professional football completely after meeting me at full speed. That's how hard I tried to hit the opponents. It was definitely a take-no-prisoners mind-set. Calling up that boiling intensity was like summoning some sort of demon from within. Only the Lord knows where that kind of hatred came from, but during those years and afterward, it lived inside me like a burning ember, and I could fan its flames almost at will.

A lot of my injuries run together now in a blur. But as I was really just getting started in my pro career, I was *not* going to let injuries keep me from getting better and better. The intense accolades and credit given to me from the fans (and coaches) drove me even further in assuring they could rely on me in the toughest of circumstances, and I began to develop an almost instinctive ability to shrug off more and more pain.

CHAPTER 13

Wars Against the Raiders and the Sullivan Family

THE 1976 SEASON saw us go 11–3, and I vividly remember the fourth game of the season against the Oakland Raiders—that bunch of blue-collar street fighters who had a very nasty reputation for being the most physical, dirtiest, cheap-shot players on the planet. They were referred to as "the inmates who ran the nuthouse" and "work-release felons who were just let out to play the game." But they were good, *real good*. Under owner Al Davis and head coach John Madden, they were defending Super Bowl champions. I mentally prepared myself for the battle with Oakland with a determination that was otherworldly. For the weeks, days, hours, and minutes as kickoff approached, I went deeper and deeper into that nutso-frenzy mind-set. I don't know how to describe it other than as some sort of self-willed transformation into a monster I had never met. My Dr. Jekyll definitely morphed into Mr. Hyde, and I couldn't even talk to my wife—much less my teammates or coaches. The only language I understood was the play call. The only noises I acknowledged were the anguished grunts of pain I inflicted on every Raiders player I hit.

I was going to face some of the toughest, most storied defensive players in the history of pro football: guys like that crazy John Matuszak, Jack "the Assassin" Tatum, and Ted "the Mad Stork" Hendricks. I was also more than anxious to knock the helmets off Phil Villapiano, George Atkinson, and Willie Brown, some of the toughest and meanest defensive players I'd ever play against. Villapiano, in particular, was one tough scrapper who loved to pick fights on the field—even on the opposing team's sideline—and I was specifically focused on him and Tatum. And I had a particular intent to try and hurt a couple of newer players, Rik Bonness and Neal Colzie, who were mouthy trash talkers. A former Alabama player, Ken Stabler, was the Raiders' lefty quarterback and he could throw long bombs like nobody who had ever played the game. Superstars Cliff Branch and Dave Casper would catch those rainbow passes. So I knew we were in for the fight of our lives.

Oakland traveled to Foxborough on October 3, 1976, and the hype around town and the country was off the charts. We had added Mike Haynes, a defensive cornerback out of Arizona State, with our fifth overall pick in the '76 draft and Tim Fox, an outstanding safety, with the 21st overall pick. He made eight interceptions that first season and averaged 13.5 yards returning punts. Coach Fairbanks also benched our quarterback, Jim Plunkett, who was traded to the San Francisco 49ers and then to Oakland where he went on to win two Super Bowls. Coach Fairbanks also chose Steve Grogan, fresh out of Kansas State in the 1975 NFL Draft, to be our starting quarterback and shifted the offensive philosophy to letting the quarterback have more latitude out there on the field in deciding what plays to call.

That was one of the best decisions he ever made as Grogan had a real nose for what was happening on the field, and he involved the linemen and the backs in the huddle discussions in determining what play to run. Grogan was not only smart and very technical, but he also was one of the toughest players to ever don a Patriots uniform. He was 6′4″, weighed about 215, and could both take and deliver a hit as hard as any guy on the field.

When I told my good friend about my autobiography, Grogan told me: "There couldn't have been a finer pair of left linemen to play behind than John Hannah and Leon Gray. Those guys were like two well-trained grizzly bears, and it gave me a great sense of confidence back in the pocket most of the time. I'd never seen a lineman blow off the line like Hog could, and man, I witnessed some epic battles out there. He was quick as a cat, strong as a yak, and smart as could be. After Coach Fairbanks started letting me have some leeway in calling plays, I learned real quick to listen to Hannah and Leon—especially—and would get Sam 'Bam' [Cunningham] and the other backs to tell me what play would work and what would not. We'd hit the huddle and jam helmets together and talk really quick. It was like I'd ask, 'Can we make the right sweep yet?' Hannah would tell me a certain left defensive guy still had some steam and he didn't feel comfortable enough yet to back off and pull, and Sam would say, 'Yeah I still can't make the full cut yet.' I'd say, 'Okay, we'll run so and so, but you guys let me know when it comes open, and we'll run it.' Or if we needed a short two or three yards, I'd ask Hannah and Leon, 'Can you split those guys?' And Hannah would respond, 'I'll try to cut him low, and if Leon will square his man off, maybe we can blow it open long enough to squeeze through.' More times than not, letting those guys guide me in certain clutch situations made the difference between a W and an L."

Our big running back, "Bam" Cunningham, had run for 666 yards in 1975, and with the focus on the running game in '76, he and Don Calhoun and Andy Johnson all went over 700 yards. Despite less reliance on the passing game, Grogan still went on to pass for 18 touchdowns, ranking him fourth overall in the league. He also scored 12 rushing touchdowns that season, which broke Johnny Lujack's and Tobin Rote's record of 11, and for almost 35 years, no other quarterback could beat that record until Cam Newton did it in 2011 with the Carolina Panthers. Between me, tight end Russ Francis, and Mike Haynes, we had three All-Pro players in 1976, and my old buddy Gray, also made the AFC's Pro-Bowl squad.

So when the Raiders hit town, we were about as confident and cohesive as a team could be and were raring to take it to them. It was about to become Armageddon. We played the game of our careers and when the last whistle blew we absolutely destroyed Oakland in a 48–17 victory. Grogan had 56 rushing yards, 165 passing yards, and three passing touchdowns. We had 296 running yards and ended up sitting on top of the world.

Unfortunately, even though we earned a wild-card spot in the postseason playoffs and would face Oakland again on December 8, 1976 on their home field, we lost that game 24–21 in a controversy that to this day is known as the "Ben Dreith Game." We went out to Oakland for the game and beat them every way a team can in the book—except for the final score. Two specific incidents happened in that game that really screwed things up. First the penalties the referees called against the Patriots were simply unbelievable, I mean, just nuts. It was clear as crystal they were looking for every tiny infraction they could use to penalize us.

It all culminated at the end of the game when they called a crazy penalty for roughing the passer on nose tackle Ray "Sugar

Bear" Hamilton. With less than a minute to play, we held a 21–17 lead, and Oakland had the ball on our 27-yard line. Hamilton was called for roughing the passer when the Raiders had been in a third-and-18 situation. Dreith was head referee in that game. Even though replay tapes clearly show Sugar Bear's contact with Stabler was only incidental and very legal, Dreith insists to this day the call was correct. As the Oakland receiver was at the 1-yard line when he missed the catch, the penalty put the Raiders near our goal line, and they ran it in for the 24–21 win.

And when they scored on that next play, there was a flag that magically appeared on the ground against us. So if they hadn't scored, they would have had another shot at the win. When they did score for the go-ahead points, we got the ball and were driving it down the field as hard and fast as we could and we made some good yardage. Just as we were getting close to field goal range, we called a run play to Cunningham, who saw the sideline marker. He had about three guys closing in on him. When he saw that he had passed the first down marker on the sideline, he stepped out of bounds. What he didn't know is that the guy holding the marker was two yards short of where the first down actually was.

Instead of gaining the first down, we were third-and-short. We were going on a long count when the Raiders defense started barking counts, which caused three or four of us to jump offside in the excitement of the moment. We thought their barking signals was actually Grogan shouting out the final count. I was one of those guys. Well, the next play we ran a short rollout pass to Russ Francis, but the ball bounced off of Russ' chest because Villapiano was holding him so much that Russ couldn't even bring his hands together. It was the most blatant holding you'll ever see in a game, but there was not a single flag thrown despite most of the refs seeing the hold in vivid detail.

There was no question in my mind or anyone else watching that those refs threw the game. It was just the worst job of officiating I have ever seen in my life. And I don't think it was coincidental that it was when Davis was trying to get a stadium built for the Raiders, and winning that playoff game was a crucial step toward making that happen. It was totally crazy, and the Raiders went on to win the Super Bowl.

Dreith never officiated another Patriots game, but that was little consolation for our Cinderella team that had otherwise demolished the '76 Raiders. I had played the game of my life. Even with all the sweat and anger I invested in doing my part to seal what should have been a certain victory, if I could have caught Dreith as he left the field or any time afterward, I swear I think I would have tried to kill him with my bare hands. I hated losing, but losing on a horribly bad call like that left me in a rage for a long, long time.

■ | | | | ■

I got selected to play in my first Pro Bowl game after that '76 season and so did Leon. When we went to San Diego for practice before the game was held in Seattle, Gene Upshaw and Art Shell, two of the most experienced offensive linemen for the Raiders, treated me and Leon like we were dogs and like we were just rookies. They said some really hurtful stuff about us losing the playoff game to the Raiders and were constantly rubbing our nose in it and disrespecting us completely. The Saturday before the game, Upshaw started in on me and Leon again and was giving us a really hard time about blowing the playoff game. And, to me and Leon's utter amazement, Jack Lambert, the tough linebacker from the Pittsburgh Steelers got in their face. "Hey! Why don't y'all just shut up?" He said, "We all know who really won that game and how you all 'won' it. Y'all didn't beat them!

They beat you soundly. Everybody knows the referees gave you that game on a platter."

What was really satisfying about hearing that from Lambert—besides having a great opposing team's star linebacker stand up and call them out—was that there were several other Pro Bowl players in the room who joined in and agreed with Jack. It felt really great that a lot of the rest of the Pro Bowlers also felt that the Patriots were the better team and should have won that play-off game against the Raiders if it hadn't been given to them by the referees.

Even though Lambert had shut Upshaw and Shell down about the Dreith game, one very serious issue arose when they breached an NFL taboo. Back then you couldn't tell anybody what you made. It was against the rules. Gene and Art were giving all the linemen a jaw full, saying how great it was to play for the Raiders and how well the franchise took care of its players. They also said they were the best and got paid the most. They called everyone out by saying, "Let's put our salary on a piece of paper and throw it in a hat. That way we're not telling people and we don't know what anybody's making. We can get an idea of what the salaries are and we can judge and see where your salary falls in relation to everybody else." The numbers were coming in: $110,000, $105,000, $98,000, $95,000, $105,000. Two numbers were called out: $40,000 and $38,500.

When we got back to the hotel room, I got a call from Leon. He said, "Hey, Hog, which one were you?" I said, "I was the $40,000. Which one were you?" He said, "I was $38,500."

We were not even making *half* of what the others guys at the Pro Bowl were making. We were just stunned. We started talking about what we were going to do, and Leon said, "You know, [agent] Howard Slusher is out here to talk to Sam [Cunningham].

Maybe we should talk to him?" So, we started talking to Slusher and agreed to hire him to try and renegotiate our contracts.

The shock of otherwise learning from the other Pro Bowl offensive players how grossly underpaid I was at $40,000 a year made me feel like I was getting duped. As I told Paul Zimmerman in the 1981 *Sports Illustrated* article, it hit me right between the eyes that "I was a dumb, immature, redneck idiot, and they stuck it to me." After learning what offensive linemen on the other teams were making during that 1977 Pro Bowl, I was disappointed and upset. When my brother, Charley, came out of Bama as an All-American defensive lineman in 1977 and the Tampa Bay Buccaneers drafted him, Slusher was the agent who negotiated Charley a bonus and contract that earned him substantially more money than I was making by a long shot, and I had already played in a Pro Bowl.

What I discovered absolutely floored me, and then I got mad...*real* mad. I was being low-balled beyond belief, and Leon was, too. My trusted friend and fellow lineman, "Big Dog" as we called him, was 6′3″ and 260 pounds and one of those guys who always had my back, and I had his. Patriots coach Bill Belichick would later say, "Leon and John Hannah—that's as good a left side as you can get." We didn't play together our rookie year because they wanted to pair us with a veteran player instead, but Leon had taught me so many things about digging down in those trenches, and he's the one who was also right there beside me my rookie year when Buck Buchanan picked me up and carried me by the armpits. The next play Leon said, "Hold your own, John. He'll wear down quick if you stay with him." Leon always pumped me up like that, even though Buchanan did thrash me more than a few times until he finally spent himself.

So after receiving that shock of learning how little both Leon and I were being paid, Page and I headed back home to a little farm I had bought in Crossville, Alabama, where I kept some cows, worked the earth, and reconnected with my roots. I was totally in my element.

Coach Fairbanks had told us to report to camp and try to renegotiate our contracts and do everything we were supposed to do until the last preseason game. I talked to Slusher, who advised, however, that we needed to stay out of camp. I told him I didn't want to stay out of camp, so we reported to try and give it the renegotiations a chance.

When Leon and I returned for summer training, we went to the final preseason game (a home contest against the Atlanta Falcons) and we still didn't have a new contract. That Friday night Leon and I got in our cars and drove home. At about 2:00 in the morning, I got a call from Coach Fairbanks, who said, "What are you doing?" I said, "I'm sleeping, Coach." He said, "I think we've got something worked out. Can you come over to my house?" I packed my stuff to report back to camp and when I got there, Leon was already there with Slusher, who says to us, "Well, boys, it's not as great as I'd like, but it's fair and it's about all we can get in this situation. Coach Fairbanks has worked really hard on this. You ought to accept it." Leon and I immediately went along with Slusher's advice.

We walked back in to talk to Coach Fairbanks and told him we appreciated his hard work and we would accept the contract we had been presented. He looked at us kind of funny and said he had to ask the Sullivans one more time, but he didn't think it would be a problem. Besides they had given him final authority over contracts. Fairbanks went upstairs to call Chuck and Billy Sullivan, and all of a sudden, we heard the son, Billy, raise his voice and start moaning, "They're going to break us, Daddy! They're going to breaks us!" Coach Fairbanks reappeared and said he was very sorry, "I don't know why. They didn't say, but they are definitely not going to agree with this contract." Leon and I got our stuff and drove straight back home.

The resolve and decision to miss the first game, then the second and third, was extremely counterproductive. Leon and I caught fiery flak from just about everybody—the coaches, players, fans, our families, and sportswriters. *The Boston Globe* absolutely raked us over the coals and threw us in the fire. We had thought by standing on our principles in a plea for fairness and equity that we would garner huge public support. We left a huge hole of experience and muscle on the left side of the line while we held out and mistakenly thought we could ransom ourselves for a much more substantial sum than what they were paying us collectively.

We were completely, totally, and 100 percent wrong.

After we missed the third game of the '77 season, we were ordered back to work by the NFL Player Relations Committee or we would risk summary dismissal and termination of the contracts we were still obligated by. I never had much respect or affection for the Patriots organization back then. From the beginning they had misled and used me, played me as a dumb redneck patsy, undersold my salary by that proverbial country mile, and certainly had taken advantage of me. When Leon and I were summoned to appear before the Player Relations Committee for a hearing in Washington, D.C., my disrespect for the tactics of the organization multiplied tenfold. The Patriots owner, Billy Sullivan, decided he was going to teach me—a dumb redneck from Alabama—another lesson about trying to mess with a franchise as strong and sophisticated as the Patriots.

Vice president, Chuck Sullivan, got up and began talking like he was an indignant preacher, then started referring to a letter that Mr. Sullivan's wife had written to *my mother* during the holdout. The tone of the letter (which I knew absolutely nothing about) was similarly indignant and said things like "I should hope that no son of mine, who had been properly raised, would ever disgrace his family by acting so selfishly toward an organization that had treated him so well." As I absorbed those words, I looked around at the other members of the committee, and one by one, they all looked absolutely mortified. Steelers president Dan Rooney looked totally horrified at what he had just heard.

I totally broke down and started crying. I stood up from my seat and went into the nearest bathroom to try and calm down. But instead of calming down, I cried even more. Ed Garvey, the executive director of the NFL's player's union, had followed me out of the room. He came in to the bathroom and said, "Those tears were a nice touch. That was some performance, John." I looked up at him with my eyes still red and watering and said, "That wasn't any performance, Ed." I never liked Garvey anyway because I thought he was all about himself and not the players. He didn't want free agency for us or anything. He wanted to protect and control the union—not the players. But Garvey relayed some sort of resolution. "They've decided you need to get back and play," he said. "And if at the end of the season you don't have a good contract with the Patriots—one that's fair and one you can accept—we'll make them trade you to another team."

Luckily it turned out that the reception from the other committee members was only a bit less hostile, and the entire ploy to embarrass me in public and cram the elitism of the organization down this poor redneck's throat and discredit my mother in the process blew up like a grenade in Billy and Chuck Sullivan's hands. Once the story was leaked, public opinion quickly swayed to me and Leon.

When we returned to play the Seattle Seahawks, there had been scores of death threats against me and Leon, and we had been assigned bodyguards. We also had to sit on opposite sides of the bench in case one gunman wanted to try and get both of us at the same time sitting together. In the third quarter, we were winning the game and I turned to my bodyguard, Louie Assad, who was standing behind me. I said, "Louie, what good is it going to do if you're standing behind me? You'll block anybody behind me that's got a gun, but what if the shot comes from the other side?" He looked down at me and said, "Well, I guess that's just your tough luck!" We laughed a second. Call it gallows humor.

Coach Fairbanks worked me and Leon like dogs in that Seahawks game, and that became par for the course. When we played the San Diego Chargers, we got a small lead and were on our own 20-yard-line. Coach ran 14 straight plays for short yardage right behind me and Leon. That gassed us. Man, I mean we were just stepping on our tongues he worked us so hard. After the game he came over to me and Leon and said, "Well, I guess you're going to be in shape now, huh, guys?" He just wore us out in that game and made us pay the price for losing so many games early in the season during our holdout. But all in all, it was good year, and our teammates accepted us back.

Slusher was able to renegotiate my contract extension for a base salary of $140,000 with additional incentives that would possibly push me over $200,000 for four more years. Leon was taken care of similarly by Slusher, but he got traded to the Houston Oilers in 1979 and ended up finishing his career in 1983 with the New Orleans Saints. When I heard about the trade, I was totally blown away. I told the press, "We just traded away our Super Bowl." I never quite got over losing my partner-in-the-trenches. Although the truth will never be known, I personally believe that trading him in 1979 was a continuation of resentment by the

Sullivan organization that a black player had stood his ground with them and made them blink and pay.

I was also voted Outstanding Lineman in the NFL that year by vote of the players. By my contract's terms, I earned a $20,000 bonus as a result. However, Leon and I did not get invited to play in the Pro Bowl that year, and I am convinced Chuck Sullivan lobbied the other team owners and coaches to shun me and Leon to make a statement that bad boys in the professional league don't get rewarded.

While I did not get rewarded, I got punished when I faced the Chicago Bears. I had hurt my knees before, but against the Bears, this one was really bad. When I was pulling and went barreling around the corner, I got cut by Bears safety Gary Fencik, a hard-nosed, tough player, and right then I knew this injury was different. After the game the Patriots' doctors and orthopedic surgeon examined me thoroughly and told me it was just another really bad sprain, but it would get better over time.

I did everything they told me to in order to rehabilitate it, but after the season was over, it just wasn't getting any better at all. I was talking to my brother, Charley, one night and told him about it. He convinced me to come to Tampa to see the Buccaneers team orthopedic surgeon, who Charley really believed in. I flew down there and when I was through with the examination, the surgeon told me that I had hyperextended my knee and badly torn the posterior cruciate ligament. He said that if the Patriots' surgeons had fixed my knee when the injury occurred, they could have sewn the ligaments back together, and my knee would have healed. But since they did not do that and so much time had elapsed since the injury (seven months or so), the tissue had atrophied. At that point the only way to fix my knee was to reroute the hamstrings to the front of the knee and work on strengthening it.

I asked the doctor what I should do, and he said the surgery still only had maybe a 50 percent chance of success after that length of time. He advised me just to keep it as strong as I could and play on it until it gives out. The Patriots' rush to get me back out on the field instead of fixing my knee unquestionably shortened my career. I had set a firm goal of playing 15 seasons, but in the end, I barely finished 13.

I was mad, but I became even more determined to not let this incident and the neglect of my injury beat me. I worked like crazy with weights and focused on keeping my weight down as I fought extremely hard to rehabilitate my knee. Occasionally, I had to use a brace when the pain would become intense, but I specifically stayed away from pain pills and narcotics because I didn't want to dull my focus and I certainly didn't want to become dependent on them to play.

When a new team orthopedic surgeon, Bert Zarins, was hired shortly after that, I went to him. "When my knee gets so bad that it's going to cripple me and I can't walk anymore," I said, "will you promise me to tell me?" He said, "I absolutely will, John." Sure enough, when the time came, he made good on that promise, one of the very few that were ever kept during my career with the Patriots.

■ | | | | ■

In the summer of 1978, Page and I had gone back to the farm in Geraldine, and while I was still in a daily relationship with God, it was still not truly based on my total love and submission to Him, but rather it was based more on my misdirected attempts to barter with Him and ask to be rewarded by staying faithful with Him. I know that may be hard to understand, but I was living in the mind-set that I continued to decide what was right for me to do and then would ask Him to bless it.

During that summer Page and I were also struggling with the realization that we were somehow unable to have children. Even though we were intimate regularly and were taking no steps to prevent pregnancy, we had been trying long enough to realize something wasn't quite right, and our inability to get pregnant was starting to become somewhat of an issue. One morning I had been praying and meditating and suddenly experienced this peace of mind that came out of nowhere. I had a vision that I just knew was the truth—Page and I were going to have two children, and it would be a son followed by a daughter. That vision was unbelievably comforting and reassuring, and I also just knew that I was not simply overcompensating for the stress about the issue or deceiving myself. Well, my son, Seth, was born almost nine months later in January 1979. Our daughter, Mary Beth, wasn't far behind him. And I remember thinking how great and mysterious God really is.

When I returned to summer camp in July of 1978, I had a new offensive line coach—Jim Ringo. He didn't interact too much with me the first couple of weeks, and it was like we were both checking each other out. He had been working with other linemen and teaching them new moves, but he hadn't done anything with me at all. Finally I went to him and asked, "Coach? Is there something wrong? Am I doing something wrong because it seems like you've been maybe ignoring me or something?" He said, "Hog, I wasn't going to come to you until you came to me." We both understood what that meant because he was the coach, and I was the player—not the other way around.

That was the beginning of a long and very successful relationship, which would grow into a lifelong friendship. Coach Ringo had an intuition that surpassed all the experience he had gained as a 10-time Pro Bowl player with the Philadelphia Eagles and Green Bay Packers. He had an uncanny ability to see into a player's head, mine in particular, and help make adjustments to technique or attitude as needed. He also knew that I was one of the players—probably the only one—who would really listen to him and play my heart out trying to follow every single recommendation from him, and it wasn't very long until I knew Ringo was precisely the coach who could teach me and lead me to be the best lineman to ever play my position.

The 1978 season was a turbulent one. Right before a preseason game against the Raiders, Darryl Stingley, our great wide receiver who was drafted with me and Cunningham, had come into camp, but he didn't have a renewal contract worked out yet. If he didn't have a signed agreement with the franchise before the Oakland game, he said he wasn't going to play. Coach Fairbanks worked with him and his lawyer, and the day before we were supposed to head to Oakland, he and Darryl worked out a verbal contract. Fairbanks gave him his word on it and persuaded Darryl to play the game, saying he would get the contract faxed out on Monday.

Stingley traveled with the team based on that understanding, and we were really glad he had gotten things worked out with the Patriots organization because everybody really liked Darryl, and he was a great player, too. Unfortunately, soon into the game, Darryl took a horrendous hit from Tatum that broke his neck and paralyzed him for the rest of his life. He was hurt so bad we didn't know if he was even going to live. It was just unbelievable how shocked we were, and there were guys crying and throwing up in the locker room over this horrible tragedy that happened to one of our favorite teammates. We found out later on that Darryl's attorney, Jack Sands, called the Patriots early Monday morning after the game and asked to have the verbal contract signed and sent to him. I think that Chuck Sullivan actually told him, "We don't have a contract with Stingley."

Coach Fairbanks was livid. He decided right then he wouldn't stay with an organization that treated its folks like that as he had given Darryl his word just like he had done to Leon and me a couple years earlier. Before the playoffs began, we were in Miami, and Coach Fairbanks announced to the team that he was leaving after the season to take the head coaching job at Colorado. We all knew why and were very understanding of the decision, even though we were sad to have him leave.

While he was talking to us, Billy Sullivan himself stormed into the locker room in a rage and basically kicked Coach Fairbanks out and told him to leave and never come back. So we went into that game fighting for the AFC East division—our first chance to beat the Miami Dolphins on the road, which the Patriots had never done—without a head coach. He appointed offensive backfield coach, Ron Erhardt, and defensive coordinator, Hank Bullough, as co-head coaches for that game. But by then, even though we were going into the game of our careers at that point, we were so utterly demoralized that we fell apart, and Miami absolutely obliterated us 23–3.

Darryl spent the rest of his life in a wheelchair. Apparently, he and Tatum never spoke after that hit, and there is some discrepancy whether Tatum ever tried to contact him. But to show you what kind of guy Darryl was—when he heard in 2003 that Tatum had lost part of a leg to diabetes, Stingley told *The Boston Globe*, "Maybe the natural reaction is to think he got what was coming to him, but I don't accept human nature as our real nature. Human nature teaches us to hate. God teaches us to love." After I heard that, I said to myself, *That one quote could just about sum up everything I had believed my whole life.*

On a more positive note, a couple of really good things happened during the 1978 season. That was the year we broke the NFL rushing record with 3,165 combined yards. What made it even more remarkable is that we didn't have a single back that ran for 1,000 yards. Instead we had five different backs that all went over 500 yards, and I have to give total credit to Coach Ringo for really pulling the entire offensive line together and making that season our best ever. I'll give you one example how he did that. There was another lineman, "Pimping Sam" Adams, who would fake an injury when he got really tired, and he'd look over at the sidelines and ask to be taken out.

We called him "Pimping Sam" because every time the team would travel or he'd be out on the town for the night, he'd wear the nicest most elegant three-piece suits you'd ever seen. The funny thing is he'd always wear ratty, old canvas tennis shoes with holes cut out along the sides because his corns and bunions hurt him so much. He was quite a sight with his combined style of Armani and Keds with holes in the sides, and we thought he looked like a street pimp, so he got the nickname "Pimping Sam" that stuck with him for his entire time with the Patriots. Coach Ringo caught on to "Pimping Sam" faking injuries real quick. He told Sam in one team meeting, "Sam, if you ever fake another injury again to get taken out for a rest, I'm going to ignore you." Well, sure enough in a late September game, we had been on an 11 or 12-play drive, and Pimp was pooped and started looking over at the sidelines. Coach Ringo actually turned his back to the line and wouldn't even watch the next few plays—much less take Sam out. From then on he never tried to fake another injury but continued to play ball instead and he got much better endurance and became an even better lineman.

In an early October 1978 home game against the San Diego Chargers, their big defensive lineman, Gary Johnson, was just killing me in the first quarter. I couldn't touch him, and he sacked Grogan several times, running over me. The more he beat me, the madder I became. The madder I got, the more he beat me.

Finally, Ringo pulled me out the game and said, "Hannah, hit the bench!" He sent in a substitute and came over to talk to me. "John, just calm down, buddy. Calm down...Nobody's better than you. The only reason you're getting beat is because you're using the wrong technique. Think about what he's doing to you and think about what techniques you can use to beat him."

It was like a huge light went on—daylight dawns on Marblehead, as they say in Massachusetts. That singular lesson Coach Ringo taught me is the top lesson I learned the entire time I was in the pros. *Nobody's better than I am; the only reason I'm getting beat is because I'm using the wrong technique.* That became my mantra from then on. Before that sound advice, my natural response to getting beat was to think the other guy was better than I was, and in order to beat him, I had to get madder and madder and play harder and harder to beat him. Coach Ringo opened up a thought process I had never used before, and it added a completely new dimension to how I approached the game of professional football.

CHAPTER 14

The Snowplow Game

THE SNOWPLOW GAME is one of the most misunderstood, controversial games in NFL history. I believe the day we played this game was the coldest I had ever been in my life. We were playing one of our rivals, the Miami Dolphins, on our home field at Schaefer Stadium just outside Boston. For an Alabama farm boy who was used to steaming hot summers, the temperature that day chilled me to the bone, even though I'd been in Boston almost nine years by then and had somehow already survived some remarkably harsh, Northern winters with even colder days.

In the days preceding that December 12, 1982 game, it had rained almost non-stop. It hadn't snowed yet because the temperatures hovered just above freezing, but still the rain was as cold and dank as it could be, and the frigid Boston air made it feel like a meat locker even without snow on the ground. There had been so much rain in the days before the game, the field at Schaefer Stadium was completely saturated.

The weather forecasters were calling for snow on gameday, but we did not know how much or hard it was actually going to snow. Frankly I think the intensity of the snowstorm actually caught everybody off guard, and even though it was coming down in huge, blinding sheets of white, the game kicked off as usual. When it became apparent it was going to accumulate heavily on the playing field, head coaches Ron Meyer (Patriots) and Don Shula (Dolphins) met and agreed to a special game rule that would allow the use of a small snowplow to come onto the field and clear the yard markers in order to give the players a general point of reference. Quickly the Patriots' maintenance crew rigged up a small John Deere lawn tractor with a spinning brush attachment normally used for clearing leaves off the field in the fall and trash debris from the stadium after home games. It saw repeated service as a snowplow to clear those yardage markers all through the game.

Despite regularly clearing the yardage lines, the game remained scoreless until deep into the fourth quarter. The ball had gotten extremely firm in the cold snow, and most receivers and backs' hands were numb, which caused many fumbles and missed passes. The ground was so slippery that the players weren't even running. They were just walking fast. It was perhaps one of the ugliest professional football games I played in my entire career. Every time a team would have to kick, the holder would try to sweep as much snow away as he could with his hands. This was necessary for the ball to be spotted firmly enough to plant in the right spot and long enough for the kicker to strike it.

With less than five minutes to go in the fourth quarter, we had finally driven the ball down to the Dolphins 33-yard line and we were within field goal range. With the snow continuing to pour, the field was a blanket of complete white. Just as our kicking team was preparing to get in position at the line, out of nowhere came the guy on the John Deere snowplow brushing the yardage markers. Matt Cavanaugh had already done his best to sweep a clean spot for the placement of his hands, but to my utter amazement, just as the snowplow driver reached nearly the center of the line he cut the ersatz snowplow left and brushed a clear swath of snow right where our holder, Matt Cavanaugh, was already getting down on one knee to hold for John Smith's field goal attempt. This part of the story is very misconstrued. In reality the tractor had not swept the exact spot where the ball was going to be placed. Instead the driver had actually thrown a whole bunch more loose snow over the spot Cav had cleared. So Cav and Smith had to quickly get down and sweep the spot clear with their hands again just in the nick of time. Bill Lenkaitis snapped the ball to Cav, who caught it and set it down perfectly for Smith, a lefty, to come sweeping in for the kick. Even in the driving snow, the kick was good and the Patriots went up 3–0.

As the kicking team ran off the field, I could see the Dolphins sideline explode on the opposite side of the field and instantly Shula was leading a charge of assistant coaches and players toward the middle of the field. They were all yelling and screaming, throwing playbooks, headsets, and helmets.

After what seemed like an eternity of argument, protests, screaming, and hollering, the game resumed, and the play stood. The Dolphins played like their hair was on fire. In the remaining few minutes, pure adrenaline pushed them within field goal range for the tie attempt. In all fairness the Dolphins were also offered the use of the snowplow by the head referee to clear the field for their kick, but with complete indignation and certainty the game would be nullified for the unfair use of it by the Patriots, Coach Shula adamantly refused to stoop to such tactics and chose to kick as the field lay.

The kick was no good, and the Patriots went on to win 3–0 in what would infamously become known as "The Snowplow Game."

Shula appealed vehemently to NFL commissioner Pete Rozelle, who ultimately decided that since there was no specific rule prohibiting the clearing of a snow-obscured field for a field goal kick, he ruled the win would stand. Shula later was said to have called it the biggest event of overt cheating he had ever witnessed in professional football. If you look closely at the game films of that play, however, you'll see exactly what I'm talking about. The snowplow didn't help us. It made the kick more difficult.

What made that game even more memorable is the guy driving the John Deere lawn tractor or snowplow was Mark Henderson, a convicted burglar who was on work release. When Shula's appeal to the NFL commissioner was rejected, Henderson became a Patriots hero, and his John Deere snowplow now hangs from the ceiling in the Patriots' Hall of Fame as a permanent exhibit.

Miami made a huge deal about the fact that the Patriots had sent in a criminal to execute another criminal act. Whenever we played Miami in Florida during the years after that game, they sold a bunch of fake plastic snowballs to the fans. The fans would pelt us with thousands of those things as we ran into the stadium.

CHAPTER 15

SI's "Best Offensive Lineman of All Time"

IN JANUARY OF 1979, my world lit up like fireworks over Boston Harbor. My son, Seth Michael, was born January 25th, 1979. His name translates to "anointed one like unto God." When Leon Gray was traded to the Houston Oilers in 1979, however, I was devastated. I began eating and drinking more, and my weight steadily climbed up toward 300 by the 1980 season. I had never lifted weights much before, but the continued injuries to my knee and ankles were made worse by carrying the extra weight, so the Patriots suggested I try weightlifting as a means to cut some of the weight off and perhaps gain back some of the quickness I had lost. I took it up and found they were right. I felt trimmer, stronger, and faster. As a result I became more confident and less angry. We had a so-so, 10–6 season that year, but shortly after that season, *Sports Illustrated* contacted my agent, Howard Slusher. They told him they wanted to do a story on me.

Any interest, of course, from the best known sports magazine on the planet was flattering, and the football image I had struggled so hard to build and sustain was about to take a huge step up in exposure. I had no idea about the story's focus, its length, or when it would run. All I knew is a staff writer, Paul Zimmerman, would be contacting my agent to make arrangements to meet and interview me. As I usually went back home to the farm in Albertville, Alabama, to decompress and see my folks and brothers after the NFL season, Zimmerman said he'd like to come to Alabama and do the story there instead of back in Boston. That was fine with me because I was finding I needed a break from Boston more and more.

So in June of 1981, Zimmerman came down from New York City and spent an entire week with me and my family in Albertville. He was an amazingly engaging fellow, and his command of sports trivia and more, particularly my own statistics, was very impressive. It was obvious he had done a huge amount of preparation and research ahead of time, but I wouldn't know until the article ran exactly how much colossal research he had done or how many people he had talked to before coming to see me. I also figured out later that he indeed had a very good handle on the vastness of my ego and had played to my vanity like the fine violin I was holding in the article's opening picture. In that regard he was a masterful interviewer and pushed every button he could to get that ego moving and shaking to give him everything and more for the article.

When the August 3rd, 1981 issue of *Sports Illustrated* was released, everything changed. My whole world exploded, and my head swelled. I had no idea it was going to be the cover feature story nor that it would proclaim me "The Best Offensive Lineman of All Time." I was absolutely and totally 100 percent blown away. The rock star, super celebrity, mega-athlete mentality washed over me. The ensuing calls, letters, media inquiries, visits, offers, sponsorships—you name it—came pouring in. In the process the real John Allen Hannah all but got squeezed out of this image. My mug was on the front of *Sports Illustrated.*

The entirety of that article is reprinted at the end of this book. I got *Sports Illustrated's* permission to include it because it is a vivid footnote and reminder of the impostor I used to be, a man bent on greatness for the sake of his self. Sprinkled throughout, though, are nuggets and clues of who really was hiding behind that helmet and shoulder pads 30 years ago, and I take satisfaction knowing that God indeed knows what He's doing, and that the Psalm 73 my life was drawn from is literally translated to "God is Good."

When I was interviewed a short time later about the article, all I could think of was, *This is going to be a very long year.* In the world of professional football back then, surviving 13 seasons as a starting offensive lineman was the exception rather than the norm. I had to fight off huge, angry defensive players like Randy White and Joe Klecko. I'm not quite sure that my old high school coach and mentor at Baylor School, Major Worsham, could have ever predicted that by teaching me agility and reactions and by slotting me on the defensive side of the line against four other offensive linemen would have ever paid off in the future like it did. But those lessons earned me nine Pro Bowl appearances, four Offensive Lineman of the Year awards, and 10 years on the All-Pro teams. It also got my picture and a huge old article in *Sports Illustrated,* which declared me "The Best Offensive Lineman of All Time."

But as I correctly predicted, it also earned me a great big bull's-eye right on the front of my No. 73 jersey. It became a mission of defensive linemen and secondary players to get through me at all cost or—if they couldn't beat my block—hurt me anyway they could. That left knee, which is long overdue for total replacement, was my main knee, the shock absorber, and the coiled spring I'd fire off of all rolled into one. There came a time in my 10th season when I knew—I just knew—that I was damaging it more and more with every down. Tape wasn't helping anymore, and the anti-inflammatory pills I was taking by the palm full hardly put a dent in the agony. I knew in my heart that it was time to quit. The rest of my body was only slightly less damaged. Had I been a car that went into the body shop for a repair estimate, I would have probably been declared totaled.

When I floated the idea to a couple of trainers and an assistant line coach about getting out, taking my disability, and collecting the rest of my contract terms in a commuted day value, word got back to the organization pretty quickly, and the response I heard back was a resounding, *"No!"* It seems the memories from 1977 of the unexpected public embarrassment when Billy Sullivan's wife had tried to shame me and my mother during my contract holdout had not been forgotten or forgiven. The interpretation of the organization's lack of concern for my physical well-being was: "He wanted a contract so bad. Well, he got one, but so did we, and we're going to make him stick to it."

That total disregard for my health and future ability to walk because my injury against the Chicago Bears had not been fixed in a timely manner was not helped by Page, my then-wife, who was not supportive of me in my desire to get out and do damage control. She had gotten used to thriving on being known around Boston and its social circles and she loved whipping out her credit card that said "Mrs. John Hannah" and having waitresses and clerks fall over her when they learned who she was. So to get along, I just had to go along...as long as I possibly could endure the pain and continuing damage to my entire frame. I have to admit now, however, that I was becoming very scared of what might happen to me if I got hit the wrong way too many times.

I dug very deep and clung to the image I had adopted, and that now defined me as one of the most respected offensive lineman in the NFL. I, though, was deathly afraid of being humiliated and tarnished from the recognition that I was "The Best Offensive Lineman of All Time." The image that I had worked so hard to build also held me hostage to my own pride and vanity. I had more surgeries. I also channeled that fear of being humiliated back into anger, a deep, abiding anger that would protect me against the physical pain and mental fear of losing control. I was going to control myself and everybody else I could as long as possible and I didn't give a hoot what I had to do to stay in control.

■ | | | | ■

1983, however, was a colossal year, for one more main reason. By now I had become totally burned out beyond belief with the mistreatment I had endured from the Sullivan organization. I was being paid about half of what linemen on other teams were getting, and none of them had built a record of high performance anywhere near what I had accomplished. I was frustrated playing under head coach Ron Meyer. I wanted to be traded. Word soon got to me that Raiders owner Al Davis was very interested in talking to me about a trade, and he was said to have stated that he really wanted a dose of the Hannah genetics and a fiery belly on his front line. He was going to do whatever it took to get me.

When I realized this was serious, I arranged a meeting with my dad, David, and Charley, who loved the Buccaneers but was having his own issues with Tampa Bay then, to meet at Vaughn's Catfish restaurant in Guntersville, Alabama, to make plans on how to approach Davis' interest in me. Charley was running late. When he finally got there a half hour later and sat down at the table, Charley looked like he had seen the devil himself. "I've been traded," he said.

If he couldn't negotiate his contract to receive a better deal, that's what Charley wanted. So we didn't understand why he looked so concerned—almost sick. "Where, Charley?" Dad asked. "Oakland," he replied. The words went off like a bomb in my ears. "You took my job, you son of a gun," I said.

"I had no idea any of this was going on," Charley said. "But I got a call from Al Davis himself, and he told me that he had been on the prowl to try and make a trade for John, but he said that Chuck Sullivan told him that he would only trade John if he got two No. 1 draft picks back to back. He said Tampa Bay only wanted one fourth-round draft pick for me. Since Davis wanted a Hannah temperament on his team regardless, he traded for me."

That was crazy. I was 34 years old, and no one is worth two No. 1 draft picks—much less a 34-year-old lineman. Charley was traded to Oakland, and then Davis did the unthinkable. Charley had always played on the right side of the line while wearing No. 76, but the Raiders moved him to left offensive guard (my position) and assigned him a uniform—with No. 73 (my number) stitched across the front and back. We played two professional games against each other, and the audacity of those team owners to manipulate us so badly in their high stakes game of one-upmanship was simply unspeakable and the most callous thing I could ever imagine.

Charley won a Super Bowl that year.

I really struggled with that betrayal and being used as a pawn. I wanted out. Right then, I decided I was going back home to help dad with Hannah Supply, which had gotten to be a major enterprise by then. Plus at age 64, Dad was ready to have some relief or sell the company if I didn't come back and take it over. When word got out that I was outraged and close to quitting, Chuck Sullivan's other son, Pat, called me and urged me to reconsider. "If you come back," Pat said, "I promise you, John, you'll never have to work another day in your life." He and the team psychiatrist came down to Alabama to talk to me in that summer of 1983. They convinced me that despite the past record of broken promises I should trust Sullivan this time because he really meant it. They offered me a substantial increase and guaranteed salaries of $200,000 in 1984 and $225,000 in 1985.

I went back and talked to Dad. He told me if the Patriots are going to pay me that much that he was going to sell Hannah Supply. But even with that raise, I found out later that Pete Brock, the starting center, was making $160,000 more than I was, and Brock and didn't even start until 1979—let alone make a Pro Bowl or receive other honors. Something still was not right about the whole situation. I told linebacker Steve Nelson what I was making. "I can't believe they screwed you like that again," he said.

■ | | | | ■

The majority of my final year with the Patriots in 1985 turned out to be less than spectacular. Although we won the AFC Championship, I earned All-Pro honors, and was again selected to play in the Pro Bowl in Hawaii, we absolutely stunk in Super Bowl XX. We were facing the Chicago Bears and were going to play in the Superdome in New Orleans on January 26, 1986. My left knee was screaming at me on a daily basis after the regular season. Deep down I was worried to death that game very well might be my last, and I was really concerned that one wrong twist or hit to my left knee might cripple me for life. But I wanted to go out a hero and blocked all the pain and fear out as I made up my mind to play the game of my career.

We got out to a quick start but lost ground from which we never recovered. Early into the game, my left knee started burning like never before. On each down, I'd get into stance, plant my left foot, and silently scream at myself, *C'mon knee, c'mon knee!*

Just one more, please! One more down! Those screams were futile, however, and play after play as I crashed into the Bears' defensive line, my knee became blazing white hot with agonizing pain, and our quarterback, Tony Eason, just couldn't make anything happen no matter what opportunities the line gave him. I, of course, have to give credit to the Bears' defense and rushers, who were playing out of their minds. Time and time again, they crashed the line and collapsed the pocket before Eason could get his arm back. Sack after sack, it was like watching a train wreck in slow motion. We actually got into minus yardage that game, which was another NFL low.

We got our clock cleaned 46–10. For a long time, I blamed our miserable loss on myself and the offensive line. I also believe we played so poorly because so many guys were worried about *The Boston Globe* article detailing drug use that we never could focus as a team.

Eventually I limped off the field after another sack, raging mad and with my shoulders throbbing because I had torn rotator cuffs in both. My shoulders were torn so badly that I couldn't raise either arm above shoulder height. I purposely walked straight by coach Ray Berry and hollered out of the corner of my mouth, "Put in Grogan! *Put in Grogan!*" I don't know if my anger or admonition was what triggered his decision, but on the next set of downs, Berry benched Eason and sent Steve (Grogan) in. Steve went in and gave it his best shot, but unfortunately it was too late, as Chicago's wrecking crew and offense under Jim McMahon was on fire and hotter than Mrs. O'Leary's cow. When the dust settled, a huge 320-pound rookie Bear named William "The Refrigerator" Perry even flopped over the Patriots' goal line after a 1-yard stumble and sealed the final score at 46–10.

It was the worst drubbing of an opponent in Super Bowl history to date.

With the physical torture to my knee and shoulders and the embarrassment of that Super Bowl loss, I thought God had let me down because I failed to pull the team through when it meant the most. Some sportswriters quickly began suggesting the loss was mainly the fault of the Patriots offensive line, which did very little to stop the defense's rush and let Eason get sacked so many times. As far as I was concerned, they were probably right. I fought the humiliation I feared by assuring myself that, even though I gave everything I had in that game and competed with such aggression despite the badly failing left knee and busted shoulders, it was absolutely the whole team's fault we lost. I became incredibly angry at everyone—and myself.

As I thought ahead to the coming season in 1986, I simply could not get my mind wrapped around the idea of another season of bruising hits and fights, 12 more months of pain and pills, and especially another year of microscopic scrutiny. My body just couldn't take it anymore. I had already pushed it to the limit and way beyond and had to force myself to admit with brutal honesty that I didn't want to risk another devastating or crippling injury or—worse—the possibility I might start the first couple of games of the '86 season but not be able to perform at peak level, then get benched, and replaced by some young gun. Nope, I wasn't going let that happen. I most assuredly was not going to risk all those years being called "the Best" only to be replaced involuntarily because I couldn't cut it anymore.

After that loss to the Bears in the Super Bowl, I had three more surgeries that spring of 1986. I had to have my left knee cut and I had a second rotator cuff surgery on both my shoulders. My multiple injuries were once called "probably the worst kept secret in all of football," and I had to face the obvious.

After the surgeries I went back to the team orthopedic surgeon, Bert Zarins, and asked him how everything looked. I reminded him of his promise to me years before and I asked, "Is my knee really that bad?" He held the X-ray up and said, "Your cartilage is powder, John. Your knee is now bone on bone." I asked him, "What does that mean?"

"If you keep on playing, you'll end up just like [Boston Bruins star] Bobby Orr," he said. "I can't tell you not to play, John, but if I were you and had another source of income where I could support my family, I'd sure be doing that instead."

Dr. Zarins would have been fired as team surgeon if he had told me I couldn't play anymore. That's the way the Sullivan family operated. Still, even though he didn't come right out and say it, he kept his promise from 1977. The message was clear as a bell and so was my decision.

I was going to go out on my terms, so it didn't take very long to announce my retirement, a decision in all honesty I had probably made just moments after the Super Bowl loss. My first wife, Page, was absolutely livid with me. She remained at a low boil from the day I announced my retirement until we divorced nine years later in 1996. She also never expressed much real respect for me most of those last years.

The Patriots had been less than honorable with their 1983 promise that if I came back to the team they would pay me so much that I would never have to work another day in my life. And because of that promise, Dad sold Hannah Supply, the family business, which he had worked most of his life to build and was going to turn over to me.

I had been working during the last few offseasons with a Boston investment banking firm, L.F. Rothschild, Unterberg, Towbin, Inc. and was offered a job to work with them full-time. Moving from a football uniform to a business suit was going to be a real transition. I was going to put professional football, the Sullivans, and the Patriots behind me forever.

CHAPTER 16

Hall of Fame Pride Comes Before the Fall

I FIND IT ODD now and somewhat sad that I completely defined my life and goals back then as a mission to become the best at playing a game. I slowly woke up and found it morbidly funny how my life during my 13 years with the Patriots was defined and driven by football metaphors, which were just gridiron-specific translations of those old words: "Don't let anybody push you around, boy!" Looking back now, my mindset for years on and off the field was always translated through competitive and confrontational terms. I had become the full impostor and was football personified. Strange thing is I never really knew how much my mind and heart were so severely stunted in the process by living large in the very small world of professional football.

For me there was nothing else. There never had been and never would be. Even after I retired and got into the business world, I almost always found my self-respect exclusively defined by who I used to be. I lived in this fantasy world, believing that somehow I had become immortal, an ageless superhero whose glory would never fade and whose image of self would never dim in the reflection of those trophies. And, if anybody bucked me, tried to push me around or get in my way, I'd bully them right back until I either got my way or ran over them.

I'll say it again with both a heartfelt confession and apology: I hurt a lot of good people and relationships acting like that. After I retired I tried very hard to totally divorce myself from football.

Page and I stayed in Boston for another 11 years. I attended the prestigious Wharton School and studied pension funds and money management. I had entered the NFL draft before I actually graduated from Alabama but always wanted to tie up that loose end. So I earned my BS in business administration at Endicott University and graduated Summa Cum Laude. I grew with the elite investment banking firm of L.F. Rothschild, Unterberg, and Towbin and learned a great deal about institutional brokerage sales and pension consulting. I wanted to become an independent, successful financial advisor and ultimately incorporate my own business, The Hannah Group. I can't deny people and other businesses were drawn to me as much for my football fame as they were by my acumen for savvy investments, but I tried to assume the latter and move somewhat away from the former.

I gradually developed a specialty in managing public entity pension and retirement funds. Investors surprised me in expressing their belief that because I had been such a powerful guard of quarterbacks and running backs that I must also be some kind of gifted genius in *guarding* their money and savings. I didn't do anything to dispel that odd segue and played it up as much as possible. Soon the funds I had under management eclipsed $2 billion. Even though my image after retirement remained defined and focused by those perceptions of football, I was making the successful transition to another image, and that was of a bull trader and guardian of a lot of money.

In 1991 just as I was almost convinced that after five years I had finally completely divorced myself from professional football and re-established my identity as John Hannah, the successful financial advisor, God had a very interesting surprise for me. I was notified that I was going to be inducted into the Football Hall of Fame in Canton, Ohio. The strides I had made to rebrand myself were almost instantly wiped out. I was like an alcoholic who had been struggling to stay sober for six years but who was forced to drink from a fire hose of booze. The unstoppable reversion to who I used to be morphed to an exponential degree when it was simultaneously announced that I was the first New England Patriots player to be inducted into the Pro Football Hall of Fame, and I was going to be the first inductee into the newly created Patriots Hall of Fame.

If that wasn't enough, since my dad had been a professional football player with the Giants, he was going to be invited and allowed to give the introductory speech at my ceremony in Canton. Before that no father had ever been honored or allowed to introduce his son into the Pro Football Hall of Fame. Everything I had worked for my entire life came into sharp focus. I was singled out for some unique and ultimate honors, and my dad was going to have the opportunity to confirm to the world how proud he was of me. And on July 27, 1991, these are the words my late father, Herb Hannah, spoke:

> Mr. Chairman, distinguished members of the Hall of Fame, ladies, and gentlemen. There has never been a father more honored than I am today. When John asked me to present him to you, it was just the greatest thing that ever happened to me. I

couldn't talk to him when he first asked me. I just froze up and turned it over to the wife. But the good Lord has blessed Coupe and me with four fine sons, four beautiful daughter-in-laws, and seven very special grandchildren.

I am so thankful that most of us are here today to be with John as he receives this most coveted honor. A special thanks to the Pro Football Hall of Fame for inviting us to share in this very special occasion, which your hospitality has just been tremendous.

It is rare that a person is recognized as being the very best at what he does. The magnitude of this award can only be put in its proper perspective when you realize that only 155 men out of 1,000 that have played the game of football have been inducted into the Hall of Fame. Early on I knew John had the qualities that greatest is made of. When he left Albertville, Alabama, for the New England Patriots 18 years ago, I told him that he could be just as good as he wanted to be. For 13 years I thought he was the very best there was at his position. When John was born, God gave him all the attributes of a great offensive guard. He had the intelligence, physical talents, a winning attitude, a friendly desire for excellence, a competitive nature, and an unusual tolerance for pain. I, like the many fans who enjoyed watching John play, will always remember him exploding into a linebacker or a defensive lineman, leading the back off-tackle around the end, or dropping back on pass protection. Always giving it 100 percent on each and every play, the intensity of his play was always by the rules of the games and without any fanfare. He just went about doing his job Sunday after Sunday as good as or better than any offensive lineman that I ever saw play the game. I am sure that John will wear this most coveted honor with respect and humility and will conduct himself in such a manner as to bring dignity and honor to the game of football.

With a tremendous amount of pride and happiness, it is my distinct pleasure to present to you one of the newest candidates for induction into the Pro Football Hall of Fame, my son, John Hannah.

As I sat there listening to my dad, I was overwhelmed to the point of tears. As he finished and my time came to rise, that's when I overheard Buck Buchanan talking to Dick Butkus behind me. But I choked back a massive lump in my throat and held at bay all of those incredible feelings and emotions that were welling up inside of me. I approached the podium and addressed the crowd:

He didn't tell you about the times he ran around the house with a switch to improve my sweep. [Laughter from the audience ensued after my joke about the switch, a willow branch used to discipline children.] God, I love football! And to be inducted into the Hall of Fame is probably the one fulfillment of a lifelong dream. You just don't know what it means to me. I remember when I was growing up in Albertville, Alabama, and Mom and Dad would take us to church, and as soon as church was over, we would fly home to try and see guys like Ray Nitschke, Gale Sayers, Dick Butkus, and all those guys play. And man, I would sit there and froth at the mouth and say, *I wonder if I will ever be good enough to play with those guys and wonder if I will ever be able to play with them.* And I remember even playing in the NFL and talking to my coach, Jim Ringo, that had played the game. I went to him one time and said, "Coach, do you think I could have played with those teams in the '60s? Do you think I was good enough?" Well, what today means to me is that I made the cut. I'm on the team and right now I have the honor of playing alongside the greatest heroes that ever played football. I also want to believe that this award means in some small way that I might have given back something to the game that has given so much to me.

First of all it has given me a talent to establish a place in this world for John Hannah. And second of all, it has allowed me to provide for a family by doing something that I truly love to do. But the greatest gift this game gave me is not the honors and the awards but the people and the lessons those people taught me. All these people were major influences in my life, and they all made me what you see before you today. I want to talk to you about Major Luke Worsham, who was my high school coach. He is the guy who really taught me and showed me what love was all about. Because he would shoulder my problems, he would always stand by me to offer me encouragement when things got tough. And when things were going awry, he would make sure he would correct me and get me right back on track. Also I want to thank a gentleman who couldn't be here today, and that is coach Paul Bryant. Coach Bryant left for me a lesson of setting lofty goals and not only that but to run life's race to reach those goals. The greatest lesson that he left with me was that you have to be your body. You've got to make it your slave if you ever want to get where you want to go.

I want to thank people like coach Chuck Fairbanks, who taught me the importance of organization and surrounding yourself with talent, so you could rely on the special gifts of others. He taught me that plans are frustrated without consultation, but with wise counsel, they are established. I want to thank people like Red Miller who was my first offensive line coach in the NFL. He told me there is no better pleasure in life than enjoying what you are doing because then you give it the best that you've got, and when you look back, you are happy with what you have done. I want to thank Jim Ringo, who is probably my favorite and best offensive line coach. Because what he taught me was you can't cling to and rely on the bases, but that you have to push on to reach the full capabilities of the talent you have been given. I want to thank people like Raymond Berry, who was my last coach with the New England Patriots. And what he taught me was the value of faith and that dreams can come true if you believe the thing is so, even though it is not, but it will be so.

I want to thank teammates like Leon Gray, Bill Lenkaitis, "Booger" Bob McKay, Andy Johnson, Sam Cunningham, Steve Grogan, Steve Nelson, and Pete Brock, and all the rest of the guys who were there to cover up when I missed my blocks. I want to thank the guys who picked me up after football was over like Joe Fallon, Steve Alpert, and John Lund, and all those guys, Howard Harrah because all these guys taught me that there are people out there that are friends and who are as close as brothers, and I thank you for it.

My family has always meant the world to me—my brothers Ron, Charley, and David. They always have been and always will be my best friends. The reason why is we have never had to prove our love for each other. As a matter of fact, when we were kids we would fight like dogs and take each other for granted. But you let somebody pick on one of the Hannah boys and you just better get ready to fight us all. I loved them, and it is always great to know that when there is a time of trouble or time of joy, there is always someone to share it with because there is nobody prouder with the other guys' success, and I am so proud of Charley and David and Ron and all that they have done and what they have accomplished in this life.

I want to thank my mom and dad because they were always there. One time my mom and dad drove to Bristol, Tennessee, to see my brother, David, play high school ball. They drove back the next day to Birmingham, Alabama, to see my brother, Charley, play football in college, and then they drove up to Cincinnati, Ohio, the day after that to watch me play. They always gave it everything they had and a little more. They never failed to show us their love. Even when they had to punish us, and although at the time it didn't feel so good, it didn't feel a whole like love, and I look back now and see the fruits that punishment yielded and I might even think that they might have used that belt a few more times. I want to thank my dad for one of the greatest lessons any man has ever learned and hope I will never forget it, and that is to never be satisfied with what you have done but always reach out and forget what lies behind and press on to what lies ahead.

To sum up and kind of tell you some other things that I can't leave out, there is my wife—Page—my kids—Seth and Mary Beth—and too many times in my career they have been left in the background when they are the ones who really deserve the praise. They taught me what it means to regard each other as more important than yourself. You know it is nice to be known now as Mary Beth's and Seth's daddy rather than as them being known as John Hannah's son and daughter.

Page, you are the Hall of Famer. You stuck by me through thick and thin when nobody else would, I can't tell you. I love you honey and I appreciate it. One other person that I can't leave out that I met while I was playing football, and that was my God and my Savior. And I want to make sure I haven't forgotten any of his benefits because He pardons all my wrongs, He heals all my

diseases, and He crowns my life with loving kind-
ness and compassion. He satisfies my desires with
good things, and my strength is always renewed.

Yes, I thank God for football, for giving me the
talent to play the greatest game that was ever created. I want to thank God for all the people who
He has brought into my life and the lessons they
taught. I want to thank God for a family, which
really understands the meaning of the family and
tries to live their lives accordingly. Thank you fans
for making this possible and thank you Football
Hall of Fame and Pro Football. Thank you for
everything, and I appreciate this great honor and
God bless you.

After my induction in 1991, I tried to return to a normal way
of life back in Boston. The pedestal I had just been elevated to,
however, and hearing my father speak those words I had longed
for all my life would become the emotional chains that would
keep me captive again to the impostor image for a very long time.

Those five years of trying to re-establish my identity after
retirement from the Patriots until my induction in 1991 were
rendered null and void. The former image I had been enslaved
to for so long and with which I had successfully moved beyond
was suddenly reignited and roared back to life, taking a renewed
presence in every aspect of my life.

Although I was living a public life of continued success, my
private life at home was crumbling. My marriage had become all
but a façade. We argued constantly about totally irrelevant things.
I began to brood and withdraw, becoming angrier with the world
than I could admit. I started drinking way too much again, and
any semblance of intimacy between us died a very certain death.

I became hugely resentful of my wife and became obsessed with past slights or hurts she had regularly flung at me during the last 10 years of our marriage. I started coming home later and later just to avoid spending any more time with her than absolutely necessary. I started going to bars for longer and longer hours, drinking with buddies and business associates until the wee hours of the night.

I also became terribly lonely, and my eye began to wander. The totality of my circumstances pushed me over the line, and I began cheating on her. I didn't think of it as cheating at all. I considered it getting even for her making my life completely miserable especially after I retired in 1986. It would not be until many, many years later that I would own up to the fact that I was primarily the one making myself miserable, tearing apart a family and wounding my children in the process. By straying even momentarily into infidelity, I unwittingly surrendered every last bit of control of who I was and ultimately gave my wife the very tool she needed to cut me apart.

Through all the emotional turmoil, however, guilt finally got to me, and I admitted my infidelity to her. She filed divorce papers the next day. We were finally divorced in 1996, and because of my adultery and other sins of egotism, I lost everything. I had to sell The Hannah Group, dispose of almost every other asset I had—except my trophies—and she got it all. The divorce was as nasty as one could ever imagine, and in the heat of one of the most contentious moments, she even played the ultimate trump card in accusing me of being so submissive and worshipful of my dad that is was likely that he had sexually molested and abused me as a child. She hit me squarely and viciously in the most vulnerable, sensitive place in my entire psyche and soiled the very thing that had motivated me: the desire to make my dad proud of me. The depravity and perverseness of that accusation in trying to taint my relationship with my father was an absolute, unadulterated act of evil, but hell hath no fury like a woman scorned. Of course, there was not a shred of truth to her suggestion, but that wicked hit emotionally demoralized and destroyed me—worse than any shot I ever took in the game. I realized then I would do whatever it took—or lose whatever I had to—in order to end our relationship.

The collateral damage from our divorce was horrendous. My wonderful children were unfortunately torn between two parents, who both loved them dearly, but as they were fairly young, their mother manipulated their emotions, and they gravitated to her defense. In many ways I blame my ex for the ensuing estrangement from my kids. However, I also admit and accept that my own actions and ego, which caused me to fight her so badly, were as much causes of our rift as anything she had done or said to them about me. In my effort to maintain control of the dissolution of our marriage at any cost and all that I had worked for, I effectively lost all control of everything that I ever had, including my children. I lost the house, all my money, and mostly everything else except my trophies. Only through God's grace many years later would I be able to make amends and start the process of reconciliation with them. The long period of silence in between was the worst heartache I've ever experienced in my life, and I wouldn't wish that kind of pain on anyone.

CHAPTER 17

Baylor Heartbreak

AFTER MY DIVORCE and the estrangement from my children and other family members, I lost many of my major clients when I had to sell my business. After that I quickly lost all interest in the financial industry, for reasons I'm still not fully sure of. In a strange way, and this may be part of my personality, having the business that I had worked so hard to grow and build taken away from me almost overnight left me feeling like that was a sign that I had been on the wrong track all along, and I needed to be doing something different.

I was asked to be a volunteer coach for the Governor's Academy football team in Byfield, Massachusetts, for several seasons. After reaching the playoffs, we won the Northeast Prep Championship. I then went to coach at Somerville High School, an inner city school, which turned out to be a complete disaster and failure. The transition took place right in the middle of a bloody rival gang war between MS 13 and H-Block, and I would sometimes have to drive into the middle of these ghettos to get some kids to take them to practice.

There was this one kid who was an extremely talented welder. He had gotten all sorts of recognition for his sculptures and art and had won awards at the annual Newport festival. I really wanted to help this kid make something of himself and to assist him in getting out of the gangs and bad streets of Boston. I took him to lunch one day and told him just that. He looked at me and replied with wisdom beyond his years. "Coach," he said, "why would I want to do that now? I got a regular check coming in every week, and if I run a little low, I just sell an eight ball or an ounce, you know, and I get by pretty good." I wanted to be able to help kids like this.

Out of the wild blue, I got a phone call in 2005 that was going to dispel some powerful old ghosts that had haunted me for 30 years. My old prep high school, the Baylor School in Chattanooga, Tennessee, the crucible of my first major failure (when I left after hitting Rex Yon in the face my junior year) got in touch with me to pitch an employment proposal. The headmaster, Bill Stacy, wanted to talk to me about coming back to Baylor as head football coach. I remained dubious. All those harsh memories and wounds of leaving Baylor after my junior year came rushing back as I remembered how misled and betrayed I had been by so many I thought were there to help me. My disbelief quickly turned to resentment as my primal instinct was to seize the moment and push them back with a roaring "Hell, no! You have *got* to be kidding me!"

Now that I had gone on to so-called greatness—despite how badly I believed I had been treated—Baylor came running back to me, wanting to honor me, and capitalize on my success and fame. I struggled with it, man. I really struggled with it. But after hashing it over at length with my dad and brothers, Charley and David (who discouraged me from going back to Baylor), I have to admit that this might have been a way of apologizing to my dad for having left Baylor all those years ago and ruining his dreams for repaying his debt to those Baylor boys who taught him how to use a slide rule in the Navy. Dad was still alive then, and I believed that if I accepted this job, I just might have a chance to recover that lost pride he once had of my unfulfilled time at Baylor. Most of all I wanted to show Baylor it had been wrong about me all those years ago. And I wanted to return to become another Luke Worsham.

Moving from Boston to Chattanooga after all those years was still a massive culture shock even for a native Southern boy. However, I grossly underestimated how arrogant my need was to meet this old ghost head on or how much I had never really gotten over the resentment and embarrassment of being so mistreated at Baylor all those years earlier.

So I took the job and moved to Chattanooga in early 2005 to become the head coach at Baylor. I'll have to say that the players were instantly drawn to me. They came together as a team like they had not done in a long, long time. Consequently, their play very quickly improved.

But even though I didn't know it yet, I had been completely lied to by the headmaster. He had promised me something he was never going to be able to deliver—the head coach's job. It came out later that he didn't have the authority to hire me in the first place and most certainly not on those assurances. Soon after I had moved onto the campus, the headmaster told me there was a problem with my becoming head coach. So he wanted me to become the offensive line coach instead. And regardless of who he might have hired as an offensive line coach, he hadn't secured the board's agreement to replace the current head coach, who was a really decent guy liked by much of the alumni and faculty.

I also took a lot of criticism for my coaching methods, and when I started using some creative practice drills to sharpen the players' ability to recognize a particular defense shift or learn how to react to an audible, some of the other coaches thought that teaching style was very counterproductive. I was running pass plays against defenses designed to stop those plays. There was a method to this. It forced the quarterback to look for his secondary receiver. It taught the secondary receivers to remain alert and move to the spot where they would be open in case the quarterback couldn't connect with his primary receiver. It seemed like great preparation for the players, but the other coaches couldn't understand my logic. They began talking behind my back and spreading rumors that I didn't know what I was doing or I didn't know how to coach worth a flip, and that I was undoing years of discipline and training that these players had otherwise gotten down to an art.

The sniping began. I was covertly, snidely, and then openly accused of being everything from an "overbearing egomaniac has-been" to a "menacing bully." Maybe I was already on the defensive when we arrived, but for whatever reasons, I was estranged by most other faculty on campus—save a few—almost from the first day. I couldn't get any information of what was going on behind closed doors and got even less help from some of Stacy's supporters who had attracted me there. I began to sense it was a combination of things, including a perceived fear by several of the board of trustees that I would consciously or subconsciously motivate the star athletes, who gravitated strongly to me, to consider going to college at Alabama instead of Tennessee, Vanderbilt, or even Tennessee-Chattanooga.

It got worse. I was sent to Birmingham, Alabama, to help run a recruiting visit designed to attract new students. Right before I left, I had been told that plans were under way to facilitate the shift to my becoming the head football coach. Since that would involve and affect the current head coach, we needed to meet as soon as I got back to put the plan together. When I got to Birmingham, however, I got a call from the headmaster's office and was asked to please not mention my becoming head coach during that recruiting visit until all the details were worked out. I was also asked to come see Stacy when I returned to discuss those details further.

So I did this great job during that recruitment trip in touting the school and encouraging the new-student prospects and their parents to give Baylor strong consideration and said what an honorable school it was, but the topic of my becoming head football coach wasn't mentioned. As I headed over to Stacy's office the next morning, I was thinking about all the diplomatic ways to announce my stepping up into the head coaching job and how to spin it so the outgoing coach, who was regarded with tremendous respect, would not be hurt.

I got to the headmaster's office, and his door was slightly ajar, so I knocked lightly and went in. He stood as he saw me approaching, "Come on in, John," he said as pleasantly as he could. But I immediately sensed something was very wrong, and when he said, "Please, have a seat, John. We need to talk," then I knew something really wrong was about to unfold. He cleared his throat and started talking. Instantly I was whisked back through time to another troubling scene where someone else was about to tell me words I didn't want to hear. However, Bill Stacy was no Paul Bryant, and this headmaster had no grasp of the full damage he was about to cause in my life. He started, "John, uh...I've made a terrible mistake here, you know... things with the board are all messed up right now, and there are misunderstandings and angry feelings all over the place, and well, it just isn't working out. We're not going to be able to make you the head coach."

I sat there dumbfounded. He went on and said something like, "We'll offer you a nice severance package and all." I almost stopped listening as this was about to become the most embarrassing moment in my life, getting fired from a high school coaching job. He hesitated for a moment and then said, "I just hate it, John. I really do. I'm so sorry." I envisioned walking over to him and pounding my fist on his desk so hard the crystal inkwell and tiffany lamp would shake. But I stayed silent.

He never really gave me a direct explanation other than generalities about "it not working out." I finally said, "Okay then, I'll start packing."

I turned, walked out the door, and headed back to my apartment. When I walked in, those next hours and days were the beginning of the most horrible time of my life—even worse than going through my divorce—because I was having my whole identity torn from me. Here I was the "Best Offensive Lineman of All Time" being fired from an assistant high school football coaching job. And to make it worse, it was at my alma mater—the place I'd run away from before in fear that I would get expelled! But no, my stupid self had to be lured back there 30 years later, so they could complete the job, and here I was being expelled again, but this time with more horrendous consequences than before because this expulsion blew up everything I had run away to achieve 30 years earlier.

Yes, I had run away the first time because I was afraid that being expelled back then would probably blow my chance to receive a college football scholarship, and God knew where else that would lead me if I succeeded the way I thought I could. Now I had gone and achieved all those things I ran away to pursue, and here I was back in the very place where it all began, and they had just destroyed everything about the image I had chased so hard, the image of the best football player I could be that got me on the front of *Sports Illustrated*. But they didn't care about that. That picture on the front of that magazine was nothing to them—nothing. That realization would soon fester in the coming months and challenge me to face the hardest opponent I had ever come up against and cause me the most difficult fight of my life with...John "Hog" Hannah. As I eventually came to realize, it was the ultimate divine sting. God was breaking me from that which I had become in order to draw me closer to Him than I ever thought possible.

One of the main things I regretted most was leaving the football players who had worked so hard to improve and better their skills. I had connected with many of them and was beginning to form a real bond with a few of them just as I had with Major Worsham. I could tell the ones who really wanted to work and who tried very hard to get better at their positions. When word got out I was leaving, a few of the other coaches and professors privately commiserated with me. But most of all, the kids, who came to me in a somewhat state of shock, were the ones who helped me the most, and I still have several of the meaningful good-bye letters of thanks I got from them and their families, which meant the world to me.

■ | | | | ■

Even though I technically resigned, the truth is I had no choice. It was either resign or be fired from the Baylor School. Less than 10 months after I was lured away from Boston, to become Baylor's head football coach, my world turned upside down. I had nowhere to go and no place to live, so I went back home to Albertville and moved in with my dad. My mom had died not long before that, and frankly I'm glad she wasn't alive to see me fall so hard. Dad was incredibly supportive, and for the next several months, he helped me through what was unquestionably the worst thing that ever happened to me—even worse than losing my first wife and hearing the unholy things she had accused my dad of doing to me and my brothers. But getting fired from a high school coaching job and especially from Baylor hit me worse than almost anything else I'd ever experienced. It was humiliating and embarrassing beyond description and put me into a funk or depression like never before.

It was like the Earth opened up a huge hole and sucked me into it. The failure tore into me and caused me to question anything and everything about myself and who I was. Ironically, it turned out to be the absolute *greatest* thing that ever happened to me because that failure finally led me back to a once-lost relationship and complete reliance on God. But I wouldn't realize that fully until several months later. Until I finally confronted the fact I was nothing more than an impostor, I felt like a complete and utter failure and began to question everything about who I was, how I thought about things, and why I thought about things in that way.

So I basically drifted from random jobs and ventures with little purpose in my life. I did some charity work and fund-raising. I started going back to church and tried to stay in touch with old friends. I even set up a charity golf tournament to help disabled or needy former pro football players. I reached out to all those guys I had known—if only to perpetuate the one thing that kept me going, and that was keeping the impostor image alive.

I also talked to myself a lot. Over a period of months, I slowly realized I was counseling myself and learning some other strengths about myself I wanted to explore. I began contemplating how people communicate with one another and get to know each other better in order to understand each other and themselves in the process. By that time Seth and Mary Beth had come back into my life, and I started talking to my son a lot more—man to man. Life was beginning to look good again. I traveled and played golf. I had forgotten how much I liked to read and often enjoyed a nice bottle of wine with fine food at home while I delved into many good books. My favorite topics were spiritual essays and philosophy.

I also learned I had a distinct flair for motivating people and began to get phone calls from friends and acquaintances asking if I would speak to a certain lunch group here, at another organization's dinner meeting there, or make an appearance at a fund-raiser to help promote various social causes. I did that for free for a while until I realized groups would actually pay me to speak. Slowly, life was starting to regain some semblance of normalcy.

I questioned every belief or truth I had ever held, including the times—and I say that in plural for a reason—when I was first saved and then reborn. I thought to myself over and over in sleepless nights, day in and day out, if I'm so close to the Lord, why in the world did He let this happen to me? Why with all I've been able to accomplish with these gifts He gave me do I feel like such a failure at this stage of my life?

The anguish I put myself through was merciless. My dad was as patient and supportive of me as any human being could have ever been, but looking back on that dark valley I was walking through, I am awed by the fact he didn't ask me to leave. I was surely driving him insane as I whipped myself and brooded about everything. I became totally withdrawn and would spend days smoldering, sometimes not smiling for days or weeks at a time. Dad, however, hung in there with me and almost always had the right thing to say at just the right moment or knew when to let me soak in silence. He would help me get through the day.

Sometimes when I could see no end in sight, I would think the despair and self-doubt were just too much to overcome and I'd think about how it just might all go away somehow. During that horribly dark time, I even dreamed that the end would come shortly and without warning, and the heartache and embarrassment would simply vanish. But as quickly as a thought like that would creep in, I'd shoo it away like a pesky gnat and try to move forward. Through it all there will never be a proper way for me to completely thank Dad for his strength, wisdom, courage, and love to stand by me after I had stumbled so hard.

As I continued to peer deeper into the darkness of my soul, I began to ask the really hard question of myself: *Who are you, John, really? At the core of the honest truth, John, your playing days are long over, long over, so who are you really now that the jersey and helmet are gone? Can you say? Do you really even know who you truly are at the heart of things? Can you describe a core personality and look yourself in the mirror and recognize an old, familiar face now that the mask is off?*

I began to think about Coach Bryant. Although I can't say that I adored and revered him the way some other players did, he did provide some memories with incredible life lessons that have stayed with me ever since. I thought about Coach Bryant and what he might tell me at this very difficult time in my life, I looked back at some old scrapbooks and ran across an editorial from the Birmingham newspaper written shortly after his death in 1983 titled "Reflections on a Hero." A couple of the paragraphs hit home like a ton of bricks:

> He was real. Not perfect, but real. And, it was this quality that opened him to people, and people to him. There was also grace, a grace that was a rare mixture of humility and pride, which allowed him to accept both victory and defeat philosophically...He was a Hero. He did not slay dragons,

but he conquered the biggest opponent he probably ever met—himself—and was freed thereafter to become the real human being that he was.

The notion that Coach Bryant had conquered his biggest opponent (himself) and was free thereafter "to become the real human being that he was" began to sink into my psyche. I also began pondering deeply why he would call me "the best offensive lineman I ever coached" after I turned pro when he in fact told me privately before the 1973 draft I wasn't good enough to play professional football. After all these years, I have come around to thinking he was trying to motivate me because he truly believed I could be the best if I tried my hardest. But, of course, it's impossible to ever know for sure.

But that one quote about Coach Bryant led me to more and more questions about who I was and who John Allen Hannah, "the real human being," was. I struggled to be brutally honest with myself. *Was I possibly my biggest opponent? Was the impostor I had become the biggest opponent and the toughest hurdle I had to overcome in finally realizing the true image God made me in?* I began to look inside myself to recall some scenarios where relationships had failed. And as I thought through them, I realized I was doing a critical self-examination of where I had gone wrong and what it was about me that caused the scenario to end with such a woeful outcome. *Who are you, John Allen Hannah?*

CHAPTER 18

Redemption and Salvation

AS THE PROCESS of trying to unravel the mess I found myself in at 55 years old—fired, out of work, no future in sight—I began trying to understand why I wasn't still the immensely successful, highly adored, retired football great that everybody had once bowed to. I began to get a serious dose of reality. Having nowhere else to turn, I also began praying in earnest. I was asking, almost demanding that God explain to me what had happened to me and why? I found my prayers almost accusatory. Looking back on it, I suppose that was an integral part of his breaking me from my old thought processes and selfish ways of how I always did things. But I also had to face the inescapable truth that I had not made anything happen. Facing the truth required me to acknowledge that I was not who I thought I was, and apparently in the eyes of many others, that was certainly not their vision of me either. I was a total impostor.

This is the point I began the transition that Asaph spoke of in Psalm 73:

> As a dream when one awakes, so when you arise,
> O Lord,

You will despise them as fantasies.
When my heart was grieved and my spirit
    embittered,
I was a senseless and ignorant;
I was a brute beast before you.
Yet, I am always with you; you hold me by my
    right hand.
You guide me with your counsel, and afterward
    take me into your glory.
Whom have I in Heaven but you? And Earth has
    nothing I desire but you.
My flesh and my heart may fail, but God is the
    strength of my heart,
And my portion forever.

In my mind and heart, those words from Psalm 73 hit me like a boulder and clearly meshed with the words about Coach Bryant not slaying dragons, but "facing his biggest opponent—himself—and thereafter being freed to become the real human being that he was" echoed through my mind a thousand times. If I would heed those words and face my biggest opponent—myself—I knew I was going to need some serious help. I was going to be up against one of the hardest-headed, most stubborn independent thinkers with the biggest ego and sense of self-worth on the planet. I wasn't ever going to be able to do it by myself.

I begged Him to lead me where He wanted me to go next and how He wanted me to get there. It meant a bruising fight with my selfish pride and a complete destruction of the false person I thought was. I yearned to finally discover what being made in his image really meant for my life—even if it exposed every mind-set and belief, which had been my strength and comfort, as a lie. I admitted my failures in remaining faithful and true to God. When

I got baptized at nine years old, I was exposed to the idea that I mattered to Him, and when I realized He had suffered and died an excruciating death for me, I took the incredibly emotional and powerfully spiritual steps to accept Christ as my savior.

Shortly after that transition and acceptance, however, while I knew I had taken Christ into my heart and soul, the buzz of youthful religious piety wore off, and life went on pretty much as usual for a country, Christian boy of 10. As I got older, I always knew God was watching over me, but nothing else changed much about the way I thought or acted except as they naturally would for an athletic boy who was moving into early manhood. I began to gain more and more confidence in my size, physical strength, and talents and thereby found greater, more gratifying acceptance in others' eyes when I excelled on the playing fields. All along I thought I was acting right and handling well the Christian principles. In reality, however, I was doing nothing more than paying lip service to my Christianity, so long as it made me look good or got me compliments and gratitude for supposedly good works.

I really wasn't handling it at all—much less handling it well. As my physical stature and accomplishments continued to grow, so did my pride and ego. And Christ's presence in my life faded in equally proportional degrees. I seemed to always put my choices first and focused more and more on my ability to control my life, accomplishments, strengths, and ability to control the lives of those around me. I mostly kept Him out of the way and only called on Him when I felt I needed Him the most to validate whatever decisions I had made.

I was kidding myself. No matter how big I got, how strong I was, or how many games I could win, I could no more control God in my life—or anybody else's—by my will. I thought like a child until I was into my 50s. As I began to absorb the undeniable truth that my life was contained in the words of Psalm 73, my internal eyes were literally opened in the midst of that darkness just as spelunkers do in the pitch black of a cave. As a result I began to see—very slowly and certainly very reluctantly at first— certain self-truths. Perhaps more importantly I began to see just as clearly certain untruths about who I was and what kind of face I had shown to other people. The face I showed to them was the one I thought they wanted to see, but it was actually a false face or an impostor face, which all humans adopt and which is discussed in the principles of the Enneagram.

I was lost. I began trying very hard to understand why those things weren't actually in place like I'd always thought and dreamed they would be—or as I must say—as I always thought and believed they should be.

I had to face it. In many ways I was a has-been. Much as I tried to resist it, I finally had to come to grips with the harsh reality that I was a fallible human being like everybody else and had some serious personality weaknesses and character flaws I had to deal with. This was an admission that I had rarely let myself contemplate—much less admit. I had to realize and confess that I had committed many sins of self-importance, egotism, vanity, and elitism. I was now finally bearing the consequences of my sins of pride, which is said to come before the fall.

Well, this time my pride and I had fallen just about as far as a man in my situation could. And, it hurt badly but to what end? Was my anger and rage going to get my job back? Would my anger make those who had fired me somehow change their minds and respect me again? Would my seething rage make a single positive difference in anything that mattered whatsoever?

Again, the answer was an undeniable no. As I stewed and brooded over the injustices I felt had been done to me, I shut down and went into seclusion, and I became powerfully depressed—

more depressed than I had ever been my entire life. In trying to work my way through the anger and depression, I even consulted a well-known attorney, who had successfully represented other high-profile sports figures in Alabama, to see if I had a case and whether I could sue Baylor on anything. Although I ultimately decided not to go that route, I did get a healthy dose of cathartic relief and release just contemplating trying to hurt them legally because of all the resultant public embarrassment and exposure I thought a lawsuit by John Hannah might cause. But I also realized that the same finger I was pointing at them would have three pointing right back at me. I just let it go. I decided that I just wasn't going to put myself through a public ordeal like that.

Oddly, however, when I finally let that go—instead of feeling defeated again like I thought I would—I quickly began to feel better. In the end analysis, I guess it was just that sense of closure that people talk about that let me get out of the mad mind-set, dust the dirt off, and get back up on my feet again. I was ready to move on. But then again, I had to stop once more and ask myself another hard set of questions. *Move on to what?* I started trying to assess my strengths. And every time I tried to compile a list, I'd start slipping and would hear that haunting question come back to me, time and time again: *Well, John Allen Hannah, if you're so darned strong in all these areas, why the heck haven't you made them all work for you? What keeps holding you back?*

I was enslaved to that image of being a tough football player and athlete. There, I said it. I finally let the thoughts turn to more questions that ran the gamut of what goes through a man's mind when he doesn't recognize who he is. This may sound crazy, but then again I suppose I had gone just a touch crazy. I was wrestling with trying to let go of the false perception of who I thought I was.

I began to recall the story of the fishermen who were not catching any fish despite their best efforts. When Christ brought them together and provided them encouragement and compassion through Himself, He gave them confidence in their efforts and the faith to try again. He stood with them, and after they accepted his call and began to fish again, their nets were so full they could barely haul them in.

Right there in the crucible of the house where my dad had talked to me about turning pro all those years ago, it hit me.

The weight of all of my past came crashing down on me. I could not see myself clearly in any of the memories. In my mind I became desperate and completely lost in my past life. Facing all those images of my impostor face was very much like staring into a thousand mirrors at a funhouse. I couldn't see the real me in a single one. The questions I'd been mulling over and over echoed like machine gun shots in my mind, and I became frightened like never before. I felt like a panicked child in a thundering windstorm full of lightning and hail. I was alone, and all the ghosts of my past were taunting me, tearing around my heart and soul and in sheer, utter terror. I let out a wail—a howl of pain so loud it shook the windows and walls.

In my mind the anguished wail became a primal scream as I pushed mightily against the stone columns of the life I had lived. As the walls were collapsing around me, I finally broke down completely and literally fell to my knees, threw my head to the ground, and cried more fervently than I ever had. Through huge, racking sobs I asked—no, begged—God to intervene and forgive me for my vanity. I confessed my wrongness and error in relying strictly on the very strengths He had bestowed upon me at birth. In heaving sobs I yelled out my prayers for Him to please forgive me and to rid me of the impostor and unchain me from what I had made myself into. I pled for Him to carry me through this fire of hell and to please, please forgive me for not honoring Him fully through all those years He graced me with fame and fortune.

After I don't know how long, my prostrations and pleas slowly subsided. I was whisked back to a place in time I had long since locked away, a time when a boy kicked my butt on the ballfield, and Dad got mad at me for not fighting back. This time, however, I heard my dad's voice with an entirely different ring to it—one of a father's love and concern for his son. He was proud at seeing his son finally and fully reborn. I was completely broken and lay there with my head on my arms and began to listen. Through my heaving breaths and pounding heart, I heard God's voice calming and reassuring me and I blinked and blinked again. Yes, his new voice within transformed and began speaking to me as somebody else—my father—and I caught my breath.

"John, I'm here," He said. "I've always been here. You, too, are my son, and I love you unconditionally. I know you've made some bad decisions along the way, but I've waited patiently for you all these years to finally reach out and take my hand and walk with me. You know I forgive you, John. You know I do. Let me guide you now because I've got a lot of great things I need you to help me with." The voice was tender but firm and full of confidence and reassurance. "Come on now, let's get you up and out of that uniform. And take that helmet off, too, boy. You've worn it long enough. People need to see what you really look like from the inside out and not vice versa."

As I continued to listen to that still, firm voice from within, a sense of relief and something like acceptance swept over me like I had never experienced before. It felt like the weight of the world was literally being lifted off my shoulders. I swear, as I began to sit up and stand, I actually felt lighter than I had in years. My neck, shoulders, and the dull pain I had gotten used to suddenly didn't hurt like they had for years. My hands began to relax and ease up from the cramped fists I had adopted way back in my youth.

I wiped away the tears from both sides of my face as I stood up. As I let out a huge sigh that seemed to last 30 seconds or more, I felt as if I had exhaled an illness I had been carrying around all my life and I got a momentary flash of John Coffey, the gentle, muscular giant in *The Green Mile,* who had the gift of healing others by taking on their sickness or sins. In that last instant, I let out a chuckle, a small laugh at what had just happened. It all seemed so clear now. Just like Coffey, that gifted childlike healer who most people were otherwise scared of and thought was evil because he was so huge and overbearing, I, John Hannah, the hulking destroyer on the playing field, needed to remove the outer image I had adopted for so long. I needed to lose the impostor personality and exhale the bad stuff from my life. I was ready to use those inner gifts of sensitivity and compassion and let them do some good things for God.

Even though I didn't have a clue what was going to happen next, I would follow God regardless. I completely let go, submitted myself to Him, and promised I would follow wherever He led me. I knew it was going to be a challenge, but I'd never backed down from a challenge and wasn't about to now—even if I was going to go up against the biggest opponent of my life—myself.

I asked Him to lead me where He wanted me to go next and how He wanted me to get there. I felt refreshed and very much alive even if it had taken a bruising fight with my pride and a complete destruction of the false person to get there. I was yearning to finally discover what being made in his image really meant for my life. I admitted the errors in my life when I met Christ but had failed to give everything over to Him and was now resolved to dedicate everything in my life to Him and to remain reconciled with my Heavenly Father, fully, finally, and forever.

We all wear the impostor face just as I did way back when I started adopting the scowl and swagger. We humans are very, very good at putting on more than just fig leaves in our lives and unfortunately we don't realize how our coping mechanisms prevent us from achieving greater spiritual clarity and harmony with our maker. Like it or not, in the end we all will face our maker, and we account for our shortcomings in not letting his true image in us shine through. My fig leaf led me to assume a false image in a sweaty uniform and helmet. But make no mistake about it. What is more important to me now about that August 1981 magazine cover is seeing in vivid detail the spiritual symbolism of me as a brooding young man playing a game with my face mostly hidden inside a mask and helmet.

It's the perfect picture of my false face and impostor image.

CHAPTER 19

Back to My Roots

AFTER STARTING MY spiritual cleansing and image recovery, quite a number of wonderful things have happened to me. I made it through the rest of the rough spots and stayed with my dad until he passed away peacefully in 2007. Unbeknownst to me—Charley, David, Mom, and Dad had set up some modest trusts for us that were not accessible until the last of them had passed on. I moved to Decatur, Alabama, and bought some farmland in rural Blount County that fits me just right. I immersed myself in learning as much about God's word as I could and began volunteering as a counselor at the Downtown Rescue Mission, a nonprofit organization serving homeless people in Huntsville, Alabama, where I met some incredible souls who had found themselves down on their luck. I learned more about God's love by listening to them rather than talking to them. We delved deeply into God's awesome love for all of us and how if we turn back to him in total submission, He will pick us right back up, help us to our feet, and walk with us as we seek his will for us in this short walk of life.

Perhaps most important of all, I reconnected with my son, Seth. After his mother and I divorced in 1996 when he was 17, we had a very strained relationship for a lot of years. That relationship eased a little as he got older, but there was still some territory to cover when he came back into my life, and I wanted God to lead me to whatever I could do to make up lost ground. So as Seth and I began reconnecting, I learned about a spiritual program for fathers and sons in Arkansas called Authentic Manhood. This faith-based session was started by Robert Lewis and focuses on a man's core identity and helps men deal with those issues by looking back at past wounds and other things that may have distorted their idea of biblical masculinity. I found that Lewis' main ministry called Men's Fraternity was hosting a father-son retreat and decided that Seth and I could do a private retreat together on our own.

Seth is an Alabama state trooper who spends as much time with me as he can. I was so pleased when I found out he wanted to do this retreat with me. We went through that intimate, soul-searching weekend on our own, and it was one of the greatest things I have ever done. Seth and I began to talk and share things on levels I had never thought we would, and I was simply amazed at what a fine man he has grown to be. We also developed a friendship that is something I cherish beyond words. I also began taking online courses at Loyola University in Chicago to get my master's degree in religious studies, and some of the studies I undertook helped me talk deeper and deeper with Seth and explore where God's will was for both of us and how important prayer and communion with God is on a daily basis.

I continued my volunteer work with the Downtown Rescue Mission and began to realize God was using those innate traits of compassion to speak through me to others and to reach into places in their souls that had been covered up to protect against the harshness of the world and the particular circumstances that had led to their misfortune. With new eyes I also saw clearly that these displaced, unfortunate people were still all made in God's image, too, and that there was a lot of goodness inside them. My conversations with them and Seth continued to reinforce the unbreakable promise of Jesus that when two or more are led by Him to discover and ask the Holy Spirit in, the stronger and more visible the Holy Spirit becomes in us. The helmet and mask we all wear to guard against revealing God's image will come off sooner or later. Through Him we can all clearly see the perfect image of what a man reconciled to God can be. I never lie down to sleep at night with the helmet and pads on, and when we die, I'm certain we will not be wearing our impostor faces any longer. The sooner we submit ourselves to the awesome power and release of a life lived in the ways of Christ, the quicker we can rid ourselves of the human need to cope by wearing an impostor face.

I have my wonderful kids, Seth and Mary Beth, back in my life. A couple of years ago, I bought a few more acres of land, and Seth and I built a farm by hand in Blountsville, Alabama, close to Decatur and Albertville, where I'm growing a fine herd of beef cattle. I put up a barn, installed fences, and cleared a whole lot of land for pastures. I put a little cabin on it, which I sometimes stay in for days at a time. While we were building the place I've named "Acres of Grace," I continued to grow my relationships with the fine folks at the Downtown Rescue Mission in Huntsville, and a thought hit me. Some of these folks I was counseling just needed a chance to get a new start; so I made them a deal. If they would build a house, maintain it, continue to live a clean and productive life, and honor God in the process, I would give them the land to build it on.

They now live in a modest, yet comfortable house just inside the main gate to the farm and watch over it for me when I have to be away. They're good people, learning to make their way in the world again, and I'm humbled God gave me the opportunity to pass some of his amazing grace on to them with the only condition that they in turn pass his grace on to others as well.

Seth and I continue to work together on establishing a retreat here on Acres of Grace for fathers and sons—much like the Authentic Manhood weekend we went through several years ago. He's married a great girl and settled down, and I gave them a few acres on the farm, too, in case they ever wanted to build a home here. When he retires from the state troopers, he and I are going to continue raising cows and finish the retreat. It's a place guys like me, who realized late in life they've been nothing but an impostor, can kick back with their own sons, do a little reading, and talk with me about shedding their own false face. Since I also love to fish, I've stocked two ponds on the farm with bass and bream and I'll take some of these guys fishing while we explore where and how they adopted their own impostor and how God loves them regardless.

I've always loved to fish. It's relaxing, exciting, and fulfilling. It's a sport, it's a chase, and for some cultures, it's a primary means of making a living. For those three guys I talked about from a long time ago, Simon-Peter, James, and John, it was a daily undertaking—a tough job with cramped hands, aches and pains, frayed and tattered nets, and often...very little bounty.

Those were Jesus' first disciples, the ones He declared "fishers of men." I finally realized the same profound truth and accepted that I had to quit relying on my best efforts alone to reach fulfillment. I had to invite Him and surrender to his will. I've witnessed that same achievement in both common and supposedly accomplished men who were using their best efforts in striving for success but who were not quite attaining fulfillment. Whether it was a manual laborer, a struggling business owner, or the CEO of a Fortune 500 company, the resulting success for each of them by completely accepting his guidance was the reward of fully loaded nets.

It's still hard work—being fishers of men—but the rewards in heaven of putting Him first and leading others to follow Him here on Earth are undeniable. You just have to put a line in the waters of humanity and offer Him up. I went fishing with a friend of mine one time and wanted to show him that I knew how to fish—specifically that I could fly fish. I brought along my best gear, but instead of waders or neoprene boots that would guarantee my footing on slick stones or muddy banks, I was wearing rubber sandals. As I got to the shore with my custom reel and pricey carbon fiber rod, I felt confident I was quickly going to snag a trophy rock striper or bass. I stepped into the clear, blue water and began to feed my line. My friend was watching from a short distance away.

As I worked the bank and moved farther into the water for better casts, I was confident in my footing. The feeling was powerfully familiar with my left knee firmly planted, right shoulder opposing, hands steady, rod straight, and heels stuck squarely in the earth. But in a flash, the muck and ooze sunk like a quagmire and dragged my left leg into the gunk almost up to my knee. I was quickly becoming trapped, and my old plant knee failed as I stumbled about, trying to recover and keep from falling completely over into the water. I knew in an instant that I was in trouble and was about to be in even more serious trouble if I actually fell. As I tried to correct the misstep, I realized why you don't wear sandals when you fly fish.

As I tried to regain my balance, my left knee, which I had relied on for so many years in the pros and had served me well, was not cooperating. Suddenly, I felt hopeless. But in that same instant, I quietly began to pray. *Oh. Jesus, I can't do this myself…*

Please, Jesus. Please! Help me. And suddenly I was free. I realized that it was only because I had surrendered my weakness and the futility of my best efforts by calling on Him that I found the strength and peace of mind, knowing that He was in control. With that awesome realization came the patience and courage to accept that I was going to be saved by Him. When I stepped on the bank, I realized I had lost my left sandal in the mire and I would probably have difficulty making it up the rest of the bank without that old sandal unless I could somehow retrieve it. But it was buried in the muck.

Then without fanfare my friend did something that surprised me. After helping me up, he silently turned and went looking, feeling around and almost diving into the lake to try and find my lost sandal. I stood there quietly as I wondered what in the world would compel someone to do such an unselfish, messy task of service for another. Losing the footwear really was no big loss as those rubber sandals were all but completely worn out from the miles I had put on them. But my friend had sensed my problem and waded knee-deep into the cold and muddy water to try and find my lost, cheap rubber sandal.

I smiled inside as I pondered what made a man offer that kind of menial service for me. Why did he try and retrieve something so simple as a cheap sandal? The Last Supper—where Jesus submitted Himself to washing his disciples' feet—literally washed over me like a wave. I knew right then that—through a missing rubber sandal and a friend who came to my help—Christ was trying to remind me again about his love for me. That love was once again revealed.

Since I can't bring back any of those trophies from my playing days to show Him, I have to be prepared—just like my friend—to let Him know that everybody else was important to me and that I tried to lead as many souls out from hiding in their own uniforms and helmets to Him. Just sitting idly by is not going to cut it. I've got a lot more to learn from the words of the bible and will practice very hard at putting them into practice every single day. He's going to want to know what I did with all the gifts and blessings He gave me. Did I share them with everyone I met or did I just "Hog" them for myself?

Even though I have a lot of aches and pains from those playing days, as do a ton of other guys, the NFL recently negotiated a settlement with the retired players' class action lawsuit of which I was a part. That settlement now sets aside $42,000,000 from the NFL over the next eight years to be paid into a newly established common good entity and fund that will be used to provide a number of benefits to retired players that we never had. These include things like career transition counseling and assistance, help with securing housing, and medical needs, among others. You know, I may just finally get my knees replaced, after all.

My uniform these days is a pair of faded jeans and cowboy boots. I have a collection of old, wide-brimmed hats I rotate, and if you look closely at my rear hip pocket, you just might detect the faint outline of a can of dip. I drive an old Dodge diesel with about 150,000 miles on it and spend as much time as I can raising my cows, getting to know all the local folk, and building the retreat. Seth helps me as much as he can, and it's just great spending time and working with my son.

I've gotten to be good friends with a number of my neighbors who are also cattle farmers and I attend a small country church where my fellow believers worship, sing, and have family-style meals a couple of times a week.

I keep three working dogs on the farm: Pete, an extraordinary Border Collie; Lucy, a Great Pyrenees; and Butkus, a Pyrenees-Mastiff-Anatolion Shepherd mix. And, yes, Butkus is named after my old idol, Dick Butkus. While Pete keeps the cows and me in check and Lucy and Butkus hunt down all the coyotes that occasionally get into the herd, Butkus is the one who almost always barrels in for the kill. When he catches one, it ain't pretty, but it's over in a matter of seconds—kind of like how ol' Dick would eradicate ball carriers. I listen to a lot of bluegrass and gospel, and on Friday nights, you'll often find me in someone's car garage beside their house where a bunch of locals gather with their guitars and fiddles and sing well into the night.

I gave up that old fiddle they pictured me with in the 1981 *Sports Illustrated* because that was just for show. Now I have a second-hand mandolin I bought along with a lesson book and I serenade my dogs and cows as I try to learn how to play it. Yeah, this is God's country, and I love it. I feel his presence all around me every day and I love staying very close to Him and his other children. I read his word several times a day. When I'm on the porch or driving the tractor, I continue to contemplate the divine power that birthed me in Psalm 73, stitched that number to my chest, and tied me to a comet that hurtled me all the way from Alabama to Boston—and back again.

Appendix

John Hannah Doesn't Fiddle Around

At least not on the football field, where, says the author, his brains, brawn and speed have made him the top offensive lineman in NFL history

By Paul Zimmerman

SEE NOW, it's starting. Ah, what a parade. Simply magnificent. All the great linemen in NFL history, the offensive linemen, those quiet, dignified toilers in anonymity. Here they come now. Look who's leading the way. Jim Parker. So big, so graceful. God was certainly generous when He created him. And see that little one snorting and pawing the ground, the one with the blood on his jersey? That's Abe Gibron. And there's the Boomer, Bob Brown. Look at those forearms. He once shattered a goalpost with one of them. And that giant blotting out the sun, that's Bob St. Clair, all 6′9″ of him. And there's Mike McCormack, tall, humble, brainy. Yes indeed, this is a parade.

What's that you say? You want to know who's the best of them? The very best? Now how can someone pick something like that? The mere act of it would be an insult to so many players who were so great in their eras. You say I must? O.K., fasten your seat belt. The greatest offensive lineman in history is playing right now and probably hasn't even reached his peak. He is John Hannah, the left guard for the New England Patriots, out of Alabama. He stands 6'2½" and his weight fluctuates between 260 and 270 (no lineman can honestly claim only one weight). He is 30 years old and is in his ninth year and is coming off the best season he ever had. He is a pure guard; he's never been anything but a left guard since he started playing in the NFL. He hasn't bounced around between guard and tackle as Parker did, or Forrest Gregg or Bob Kuechenberg; never had to go the offense-defense route like McCormack and Gibron and Chuck Bednarik.

Is it sacrilege to pick a current performer as the greatest who ever lived, in anything? Greatest actor, chef, rodeo rider? Should we wait until he's retired and enshrined and halfway forgotten? Weeb Ewbank, the former coach of the Baltimore Colts and New York Jets, thinks so. "Back off a little, give it some historical perspective," he says. "Let John make the Hall of Fame first."

Weeb's man is Parker, whom he coached for six years in Baltimore. Parker is also the choice of most of the coaches and personnel men who have been around the NFL for a few decades. McCormack generates surprising support, particularly from the Cleveland Browns' faction. Gibron is a dark horse. Don Shula, who coached Parker for five years and has coached against Hannah for eight, gives Parker a slight edge, but then he whispers, "Don't forget about our own guy, Bob Kuechenberg." Hannah's line coach, Jim Ringo, favors a troika of Hannah, Parker and his old Green Bay teammate, Jerry Kramer, but some people feel that although Kramer and Right Tackle Forrest Gregg were legitimate superstars, they fell under the category of a perfect mesh in a perfect offensive line. The big-name centers of the past—Mel

Hein, Frank Gatski, Bulldog Turner, Bednarik, Ringo—receive little support. The opinion is that guards and tackles work in a less protected environment. Only George Halas might remember Cal Hubbard, the legendary giant of the 1920s, and Halas isn't returning phone calls.

But Hannah has his following. Former Denver coach Red Miller says he's the man. So does John Madden, who coached against Hannah when he was with the Raiders. Parker says, "Hannah's the only offensive lineman I enjoy watching these days." New England General Manager Bucko Kilroy, one of the pioneers of modern scouting, who has been rating and evaluating players ever since he lined up against Bronko Nagurski in 1943, says Hannah and McCormack are the only offensive linemen to whom he'd award a perfect "9."

It starts with the firepower, with Hannah's legs, incredibly massive chunks of concrete. "Once we measured John's thighs, and they were 33 inches," says Hannah's wife, Page, a slim ash blonde. "I said, 'I can't bear it. They're bigger than my bust.'"

The ability to explode into an opponent and drive him five yards back was what first attracted the college recruiters to Albertville, Ala., where Hannah grew up and played his final year of high school ball. It's the first thing you look for, if you're building a running game. Hannah says he always had that ability, but it was his first coach at Baylor School for Boys in Chattanooga, a tough, wiry, prematurely gray World War II veteran named Major Luke Worsham, who taught him how to zero in on a target, to aim for the numbers with his helmet, to keep his eyes open and his tail low. Next came the quick feet. Forget about pass blocking if you can't dance. Worsham helped there, too.

"Oddly enough," Hannah says, "he helped me develop agility and reactions by putting me on defense in a four-on-one drill.

You'd work against a whole side of an offensive line. It was the most terrible thing in the world. If the guard blocked down you knew you'd better close the gap and lower your shoulder. If the end came down and the guard came out, buddy, you grabbed dirt because you knew a trap was coming."

"For all his size and explosiveness and straight-ahead speed," Kilroy says, "John has something none of the others ever had, and that's phenomenal, repeat, phenomenal lateral agility and balance, the same as defensive backs. You'll watch his man stunt around the opposite end, and John will just stay with him. He'll slide along like a toe dancer, a tippy-toe. And that's a 270-pound man doing that, a guy capable of positively annihilating an opponent playing him straight up."

Hannah's credentials include five consecutive years on the combined AFC-NFC All-Pro team. He missed in his first three years, when the Patriots were a weak team and he was struggling to get out of the Alabama four-point Wishbone stance and master the intricacies of pass blocking. By contrast, Parker made All-Pro his second season and for seven straight years thereafter, dropping off in his last two, when his legs started going. The NFL players have voted Hannah Most Valuable Offensive Lineman in each of the four years the award has been in existence, including the 1977 season, when the coaches failed to select him for the Pro Bowl squad. That was the season he and Leon Gray, who played alongside him at left tackle, staged their celebrated contract holdout and missed the first three games of the season, an event that seemed to bother the coaches a lot more than the players. "Bad little boys in the NFL don't get picked to the Pro Bowl," Hannah said.

Parker, 47 years old now and the owner of a successful liquor store in Baltimore, says he's only gone to three games since he retired in 1967. "I get so flustered watching football nowadays," he says, "so carried away by watching guys making $100,000 a year and making so many mistakes in technique. I get so upset that I wake up with a headache the next morning from banging my head all night in my sleep. But I like to watch Hannah play. He's the only one out there who can do it all—every aspect. I pray to God that he doesn't get hurt, but the way he plays football I don't think he will, because he gives it everything he has. If you want me to rate myself, compared to him, I'll say that I sure would have enjoyed playing alongside him. We would have been hell on that side of the line. I always thought my best games were at tackle, not guard. The only comparison I can make between us is that I made All-Pro for eight years and he's got to accomplish that. The way he's going, I think he will.

"I see some things in him that remind me of myself, the way he teases 'em on plays going the opposite way, the way he changes his style on aggressive pass blocking. One time he'll fire out, the next time he'll sit back, lazy, and make 'em think it's a regular pass and then—pow! He'll pop 'em. And on the running plays he's big enough to beat the hell out of them. I've seen him beat them right down into the ground. That's the joy of it, the joy I got out of it."

The joy of being even bigger in a big man's game. And quicker. The joy of being a superior athlete. Parker and Hannah were both gifted in other sports. They were both wrestlers. Parker was a mid-America champion. Hannah won the National Prep Championship and was unbeaten as a freshman at Alabama, before he quit wrestling because it was cutting into spring football. Parker did some amateur boxing before he went to Ohio State; he says he received offers from the Rocky Marciano group to turn pro. Hannah was a three-year letterman in the shot and discus at Alabama and his 61'5" toss in the shotput was a school record at the time.

"He didn't even work at track," says his brother Charles, an offensive tackle for the Tampa Bay Buccaneers. "He'd just show up for the meets. There were so many things he could do. At that time he might have been the greatest large athlete in the world."

The scouts were noting his numbers carefully. In the spring of Hannah's junior year, Bear Bryant, in an unaccustomed moment of generosity, let the CEPO combine scout onto the campus to time him in the 40 at the end of a track workout. Hannah weighed 305 pounds. He finished the last five yards falling on his face. "I apologized to the scout for being fat and out of shape," he says. "The guy said, 'Don't apologize. You just ran a 4.85.'"

At a Hula Bowl workout after Hannah's senior year, John Madden was overheard saying casually. "You know, the best player I've seen out here is John Hannah." That observation was widely quoted but Madden never regretted the remark. In fact, he repeated the sentiment several years later at a league meeting, on a questionnaire which asked: "If you were to start a new franchise and you could pick one player in the NFL to start your team with, whom would you pick?" Without hesitating Madden wrote "John Hannah."

"The thing I always liked about Hannah," says Madden, "is that he has that defensive player's attitude, that same aggression. There's no rule that says an offensive player has to have that milder kind of personality, although most of them seem to. I've heard that when you tend to go after people aggressively, like Hannah does, it hurts your pass blocking, and I looked for that weakness in Hannah. But I never saw it, except maybe in his first year or so."

Dick Steinberg, a Patriot scout when Hannah was coming out of college, and now the club's player personnel director, says that when he first started scouting Hannah, "all you saw was that raw power. Boom, the shot, and then he'd be scrambling on all fours." Steinberg's first direct contact with Hannah came at the Hula Bowl. "I ran into him in the lobby of the Surfrider Hotel in between practices and sat him down and gave him a little quiz we used to give," Steinberg says. "There was a lot of noise, a lot of people running around every which way. They'd wave at him, he'd wave back. He was sweating like hell. He apologized because he'd been up late the night before. But he was the only guy who answered every question in the time allotted. His IQ was very high. If you look at the great offensive linemen in history you'll find that they were all smart people."

New England, picking fourth, in the first round, drafted Hannah, right after Philadelphia had chosen another offensive lineman, Texas' Jerry Sisemore. He reported to the Pats' mini-camp that March in Tampa and ran a 4.8 on grass. "I remember we were all shocked," says Patriot Coach Ron Ehrhardt, who was then the backfield coach. "That's all we talked about that night, this big guy coming down the runway and, bang, hitting the clock in 4.8."

■ | | | | ■

It is 8:30 P.M. in Crossville, Ala. Hannah's 253-acre cattle and chicken farm is here, 15 miles northeast of Albertville, on a plateau in the Sand Mountain range. It's bedtime for the little Hannahs, nine-month-old Mary Beth and 2½-year-old Seth, except that Seth has no such plans. He's giving a graphic demonstration of what is known as bloodlines.

Seth is running wind sprints—through an obstacle course of chairs and toys. He weighs 37 pounds, not extraordinarily big ("John weighed that when he was a year old," says Page Hannah. "He was very fat"), but sturdy enough, very solid through the shoulders and chest, big in the legs, like his daddy. He is running at top speed, all out, but under complete control, with absolutely perfect balance. There's not a trace of a wobble. Every now and then he stops and throws back his head and lets out a loud roar. The Hannahs watch him, waiting for the motor to run down. It shows no signs of it. He turns his head to look at his daddy, and then runs smack into a high chair, bop, forehead first. He blinks, shakes his head and starts running again. "An offensive guard for sure," Page Hannah says.

The blood of two generations of linemen runs through Seth's veins. There's grandpa Herb, who came up to the New York Giants from a Georgia dairy farm in 1951 as a 30-year-old rookie and won the starting offensive right tackle spot on a team that finished one game out of the playoffs. There was Herb's late brother, Bill, a starting guard for Alabama. And there are John's two younger brothers, Charles, the Tampa Bay tackle, and David, who started at defensive tackle for Alabama. Three knee operations cost him a pro career.

An athletic lineage is just one of the similarities in the backgrounds of many of the keynote offensive linemen. They all had speed, they all had high intelligence. And none of them was especially interested in lifting weights, either because they didn't believe in it or because it wasn't fashionable at the time.

"I always felt that wrestling helped me more than weightlifting," Parker says. He was a fully grown 6'3" and weighed 248 when he came out of high school. "I was always more interested in agility than strength."

"For us, weights were taboo," McCormack says. "It was the old traditional idea about getting yourself muscle-bound, just like those ideas about swimming being no good because it would loosen your muscles, or the evils of drinking water during a workout because it would give you cramps. I was a big man in those days, 6'4", 250. Now I'd be just average, or maybe even small."

Hannah, who weighed 11 pounds at birth and 150 by the time he reached the fifth grade ("I was just a big fat kid who looked like a balloon"), played at 230 at Baylor School for Boys. A picture in the Baylor yearbook shows him as a very imposing-looking sophomore wrestler, built much as he is now, bulky rather than fat. That was the year he won the prep championship.

Weightlifting is something he got into only a year or so ago, and then he did it to keep his weight down. He was coming off knee and ankle injuries that limited his effectiveness in 1979 and forced the Patriots to cut back on a lot of their running plays. Their rushing yardage had dropped from an alltime NFL record of 3,165 yards in 1978 to 2,252 in '79 (trading Gray to Houston didn't help), and they suggested that Hannah keep himself lighter to save his legs from the pounding they'd get on the Schaefer Stadium artificial turf. He says the weights made him feel tighter and quicker. Last year his game-day weight, which in other years has been as high as 270, never went over 261, and he played as light as 255. It was his best year in football. He showed up at this spring's mini-camp in May at 265 and ran a 4.85 forty.

Hannah had built his strength through work—farm work and heavy equipment work at the family farm-supply business. Parker held down three jobs after school as a high school senior. Kramer grew up bucking bales in the Idaho hayfields; McCormack worked in a lumberyard in Kansas City when he was a youngster; in the summer he'd follow the wheat harvest. Gibron held down a job on a section gang when he was a kid. "I worked in construction all my life," he says. "A lot of people don't realize it, but we were doing almost the same things on the job that kids do in the gym these days. You work on a cement gang all day long, you're doing a lot of 500- and 600-pound dead lifts. You carry a hod up a ladder while you're holding onto the ladder with one hand, well, you're doing one-arm dead lifts.

And even in the pros, we were always doing strength-type things. We'd go out at night and instead of chasing broads we'd get a six-pack and then arm-wrestle all night long."

Another thing the great ones have in common: When they first came up, pass blocking was a mystery.

"I started in my first exhibition game with the Browns," Parker says. "It was against the Bears. Here I was, just a few days out of the All-Star camp and I was going up against Doug Atkins and Earl Leggett. We threw 47 passes that night. In my three years at Ohio State we'd thrown 27 passes, and half of them were just throwaways... 'Just throw it deep down the field so they'll think we've got a passing attack,' Woody Hayes would say. Leggett and Atkins humiliated me all night long. They were driving me 15 yards past John Unitas. They were laughing at me and calling me 'Buckeye.' The game was played in Cincinnati and when it was finally over I told Weeb, 'You can just turn me loose here, and I'll get back to Columbus. Don't even take me back to camp.'"

Hannah's moment of truth came in the second regular-season game his rookie year when he faced the Chiefs' 6'7", 275-pound Buck Buchanan. "He said, 'Home Boy, I'm gonna welcome you to the NFL,'" Hannah recalls. "He's from Bessemer, Alabama. One time he actually picked me up and threw me. No one had ever done that before. Then I started trying to cut him and he just stepped over me—or on me."

It was a miserable year for Hannah, in all areas. He came to the Patriots "with a head so fat I couldn't fit it through the door." He split up with his wife for six months. He'd go out at night looking for trouble. His car was stolen and then he banged up his roommate's. He liked the NFL, but he didn't much like Foxboro.

Before long, however, he settled down. He gives a lot of credit to religion, to rediscovering Christ with Page. He started getting his life in order. On the field he was picking up tricks to go with his raw power and great natural quickness.

"I got films of some of the other offensive linemen and tried to study them," he says. "I tried to copy Kuechenberg because I thought my style would be suited to his. I also tried to copy Randy Rasmussen of the Jets because we were built similarly, the same wide base. He's got to get some low-top shoes, though. Those high-tops...."

"I studied my opponents. Ernie Holmes of the Steelers, for instance, hated to be cut. So I cut him four or five times. He'd get so mad he'd just keep going for me and forget about the ball carrier. He'd beat me up but he wouldn't make many tackles.

"One thing I found out was that the guy you'd see on film wasn't always the same player you'd meet on the field. If they thought you were one of the best, they'd get all fired up and play over their heads, just like teams when they go up against the Steelers. They all seemed to try to use more movement against me. If they did use muscle, it was always set up by movement.

"There was a certain amount of fear I took into the games. Not physical fear, but the fear of being humiliated, being made to look bad. The worst thing is to get beat early. That fires a guy up. A guy like Coy Bacon, for instance. He just goes wild if he gets to the passer early.

"Having Leon Gray next to me all those years helped so much. We got to know what each of us could do. We ate together, studied films together. I knew the air he breathed." Off the field Hannah and Gray shared an interest in music even though their talents in that sphere weren't as well matched. Gray was accomplished on the trumpet well before he started playing football as a senior in high school. Hannah only took up the country fiddle a few years ago, teaching himself how to play from books. But as friends will attest, he's no All-Pro with a bow. "When the Patriots traded Leon... well, I never wanted to sign another contract with them," says Hannah. "I still haven't gotten over it."

Everyone has a showpiece game that he frames and nails to the wall. Hannah's came against the Cowboys' Randy White in 1978. The coaches still talk about it in Foxboro. But Hannah says he's had his share of bad ones, too. "Oh, Alan Page gave me a rough time one year," he says. "And Gary Johnson of the Chargers. He got by me one time and he had a clear shot at Steve Grogan, so I tackled him. The ref threw the flag. I said, 'Gee, I'm glad you did that. For a minute I thought I was going to get away with something.' The ref started laughing. He thought that was the funniest thing he had ever heard.

"No matter how good you are you're going to have one or two bad games every year. All you can do is take it calmly and think about technique and fundamentals and try to get yourself together. Joe Klecko of the Jets gave me a bad time two years ago. I was sitting back on my heels too much. Last year I had a rough one against Larry Brooks of the Rams. And Larry Pillers of the 49ers—in the mud. That game made me change my style. I realized you can't fire out so much on a muddy field. Pillers was just sitting there waiting for me."

Ehrhardt likes to run films of Hannah leading the sweeps. "You see people taking a dive to get out of his way," the coach says. "You'll see John clear out a cornerback, then a safety, and he'll just continue on. He won't leave his feet. Sometimes he'll just stick out a big paw and swat 'em out of the way. He thinks on his feet, too. He doesn't make any wrong choices. He knows exactly which man to concentrate on and which one isn't in position to make the play."

"Mack Herron taught me to hit on sweeps," Hannah says. "He'd sit back there behind me and touch my hip so I knew where he was, and vice-versa. He told me that if I couldn't reach out and touch a defensive guy with my hand, then he wasn't in position to make the play. Andy Johnson ran like that, too. He and I got it down to a science. Vagas Ferguson is learning it. Horace Ivory still has to learn. He's got so much speed he always wants to run to daylight.

"I used to have trouble with defensive backs coming up quick and cutting me. Now what I do is lower my shoulder and get down low with them. If they're going to go low on you, you've got to make them pay for it."

Hannah's father has some films of John's early games. They go back to the fourth grade. "We laugh when we look at them now," he says. "John came waddling out on the field and looked like a penguin." But Herb Hannah filmed some of his son's high school games, too, and he says that when he ran them over, "I saw John doing some miraculous things. One time he was running in front of the ballcarrier, and a defensive guy came up and knocked his legs down. John just stuck out an arm and pushed up off the ground and he was back running in full stride. It's something to see the way he went after a linebacker. He'd cover those three or four yards so fast... he was into him before the guy could even get set. John would have that three-yard advantage nullified right away. At every stage in which he played, I thought he was the best I'd ever seen."

The people who give Hannah the advantage over Parker in the head-to-head matchup point to that extra dimension-- the agility and body control downfield that have allowed the Patriots to build more of a running game around Hannah than any club has ever done around a single offensive lineman. Parker was devastating on in-line blocking and short traps, but he wasn't primarily known as a pulling guard, maybe because he was almost 30 years old when he moved inside from tackle.

Very few players have faced both Parker and Hannah because there's a five-year gap between the end of one's career and the start of the other's. The closest anyone came to going against both in their prime was Mike Curtis, who played linebacker for the Colts in Parker's last three years, facing him every day in practice, and was also around during Hannah's first six years. Curtis gives a slight nod to Parker.

"It's a bitch to compare the two," says Curtis, who sells commercial real estate in the Washington area. "If he wanted to, Jim could collapse the whole side of a line. I never saw anybody he couldn't block. He was a good holder, too. Both had about the same speed and same intensity. Hannah maybe was more consistent, and I'm not trying to be derogatory to Jim. One time in practice I thought Jim was loafing around too much, so I came across the line and gave him a couple of shots. He came right after me and just crushed me. I was young then. I hadn't learned yet about sleeping dogs.

"Jim was so big and strong naturally. I think he had more upper body strength than John. If I look back and think of both of them setting up for pass protection I see Jim setting up quicker. And Jim would improvise more; he was more of an open ballplayer. Hannah was a machine, a highly trained player. Of course that could be coaching.

"You've got to look at who they played against. Parker probably played against guys who were shorter and not as quick, but they played with more intensity. But if Jim were playing now, his own intensity level would probably be higher and he'd control 'em the same way. That's the difference between the ballplayers then and now—the intensity. It sounds trite, doesn't it, kind of old, talking like that now?"

Curtis was asked if he still goes to Colt games and he shook his head. "I don't enjoy watching mediocrity," he said, "average players who bitch if they don't make All-Pro and then figure that after three years in the league they're the greatest. I didn't enjoy playing against them, either. That was one thing I liked about playing against Hannah. If you beat him, at least you beat somebody. He was after you so quick. You'd have to react and get to the hole right away or you were a dead pigeon."

He paused. "There's another aspect to this Hannah-Parker thing," he said. "We haven't mentioned camaraderie. Parker was very good for the team, very good for his teammates, and I don't know how Hannah is with his teammates. I'm talking about guys you can rely on, now. Didn't he hold out for three games one year?"

Yes he did and it brought the wrath of every moralist from Attleboro to Swampscott down on Hannah's head. There are, as the judge would say, mitigating circumstances.

When Hannah joined the Patriots in 1973 he had very vague ideas about how much a 22-year-old should earn but he knew the value of money. His father had built up the family business, Hannah Supply Co., from nothing, and he didn't do it by tossing dollars away. His own rookie contract with the Giants in 1951 was for $6,000, plus $600 in bonuses, and that was very good money back in those days. After the '73 draft John was in New England for a banquet and the Patriot coach, Chuck Fairbanks, invited him and his wife to step into his office to talk about a contract.

"He told us to keep it strictly confidential," Hannah says, "and then he offered a $20,000 bonus and a three-year contract for $25,000, $27,500 and $30,000. That's a lot of money for Albertville, Alabama, but I knew a first-round draft choice was worth more. I looked at my wife, and she looked at me. Then I decided I'd better get me an agent."

Hannah's first agent, Mike Carroll from Gloucester, Mass., negotiated a contract for four years, at $30,000, $35,000, $40,000 and $46,000, plus a deferred $55,000 bonus. Hannah knew that those numbers were low, but he didn't feel like getting into a contract squabble.

"That's one thing I always resented about Bear Bryant, that he never gave me any guidance on a contract," Hannah says. "Before the draft he told me, 'You won't have to worry about getting a lawyer. You won't get drafted that high.'"

In 1974 Hannah wanted an advance of $30,000, to be used as a donation to the Big Oak Boys Ranch in Glencoe, Ala., a refuge for children from broken homes. The club gave it to him. Part of it was from his deferred bonus, part of it as an additional bonus to extend his contract for three more years—through 1979, with an option for 1980—at $65,000, $65,000 and $70,000. They now had Hannah wrapped up for six seasons, and while they were telling everyone they had, potentially, the greatest offensive lineman in the game, they were paying him peanuts. "Don't worry," he was told in '74. "Your salary will be upgraded if you rank with the top linemen in the league."

"I was," Hannah says, "a dumb, immature, rednecked idiot, and they stuck it to me."

He kept quiet for three years. His salary was never upgraded. At his first Pro Bowl, after the '76 season, he found out what other linemen were making. "I nearly cried," he said. Charley Hannah, drafted in the third round by Tampa Bay in '77, was signed for more money than his All-Pro brother was making. John reminded the Patriots about their promise to upgrade his salary. They didn't remember it. He reminded them again. They told him to see them after the '77 season. So he walked—with

Leon Gray, who was having similar problems. They missed the first three games of the year, then were ordered back to work by a newly formed NFL Player Club Relations committee, which also ordered both sides to resume good-faith bargaining. In 1978, with Howard Slusher now negotiating his contract, Hannah signed for four years for a reported base of $140,000 each year and "easily attainable" incentives designed to get him up over $200,000.

Hannah and Gray got little sympathy while they were out. *The Boston Globe* printed a reader's parody of the 23rd Psalm, a slap at Hannah's deep religious convictions: "He restoreth my Greed. He leadeth me in the path of hypocrites for his own gain. Yea, though I abandon all honor, I fear no conscience."

When Hannah showed up at the Player Club Relations committee hearing in Washington, D.C., the Patriots had a little surprise for him. Chuck Sullivan, the club's vice-president, began to discuss a letter which owner Billy Sullivan's wife had sent John's mother in Alabama. It was along the lines of "I wouldn't want a son of mine to show such disdain for what is right," etc.

"The thing backfired," Hannah said. "I broke down completely and cried. Wellington Mara just shook his head and stared at the table. My dad had played for him. Dan Rooney was horrified. Len Hauss of the Redskins looked embarrassed. I had to excuse myself and go to the bathroom to try to get myself back together, and Ed Garvey came in there and said, 'Great performance, John!' I said. 'Dammit, I broke down. I flat broke down. It wasn't a performance.' Then I broke down again."

What the letter had done was firm up the Hannah family and place them solidly in John's corner. You have to understand this about the Hannahs. They are very close. Herb Hannah and his wife, Geneva, nicknamed Coupe, are proud of their sons (Ron, the oldest and the only non-football player, is the accountant for Hannah Supply), but they are not in awe of their football achievements. They see things through twinkling eyes, never losing sight of the humor in this world, and they express things in a wry and cryptic style.

"Can you imagine me up in New York with the Giants?" Herb Hannah says, "A country boy from Alabama. I remember Bill Stribling and me ... he was an end from Mississippi ... taking the subway one day and ending up in Queens. I was always getting lost on the subway. Anyway, we stepped out there in Queens, and everyone was speaking Spanish, and Bill said, 'Herb, this thing's done carried us to a foreign country. Let's get on it and get back.'"

All the Hannah boys work for Hannah Supply and John and Charley will continue to do so when their NFL careers are over. The company has six warehouses; it distributes through seven states in the South. John is the management equipment director and troubleshooter. His office overlooks the Albertville warehouse, and he isn't above driving 50 miles to make sure that Hannah Supply is installing the wiring correctly in a chicken house.

Members of the family are in constant touch. When Charley made the switch from defense to offense with the Bucs, he called John once a week.

"Sometimes we'd have two-hour conversations," John says. "I'd be telling him stuff and I'd say, 'Get on the floor,' and I'd get down in my stance with the phone in my ear, and so would he, and I'd say, 'O.K., now let's work on the crossover step.' Page would watch me, and Charles' wife, Margaret Anne, would watch him, and Page would say, 'What is this, telephone football?'"

John has never hidden his dislike of the New England organization. This spring, when a story broke out of Foxboro that he was considering a future job with the club, he laughed. "Just someone making something up," he said.

Like the giant Antaeus, he gets his strength from the earth—those 253 acres of it, 75 planted in feed crops, the rest devoted to livestock. He raises chickens, 43,000 at a time, in two houses. He has a bull and three cows of his own, and a herd of 134 Holstein cattle that he's raising for a breeder in Tampa. Someday he'll have his own herd of Santa Gertrudis, a Shorthorn-Brahman crossbreed developed in Texas. "Only registered stock," he says. "I'll have 100 to 120 brood cows, three or four good-quality bulls. I'll raise the calves to 500 or 600 pounds and then we'll have production sales, our own auction, closed sales; I'll go in with two more breeders like myself who want to upgrade the Santa Gertrudis stock."

The farm is set in rolling foothills. There's a pond as you enter, mink and deer in the woods. The house stands on a treeless knoll in the middle of the property, a stark, striking, sharply defined house, a Grant Wood painting.

"When I was holding out," Hannah says, "they said up in Boston, 'Well, I guess you'll go back home and slop those hogs for a while.' I think you can see that I've got a lot more going for me than that down here."

It is a Saturday afternoon in June, and the temperature is in the 90s. Hannah has just finished inspecting his chickens and trimming weeds around half a mile of electric fencing. His shirt is black with sweat, and he sits on the ground, his back against a wooden fence, watching his 2,200-pound Santa Gertrudis bull.

The bull is walking slowly to the water trough, the rich red-brown of his hide gleaming in the afternoon sun, his hindquarters swaying gently, the huge muscles of his shoulders bunching and relaxing. He seems longer than a bull should be, more like a mini-locomotive. His hind legs seem different, too, bulging with heavy muscles, instead of tapering. A gentle, magnificent animal. The three heifers at the trough slide sideways to let him through, and then stare at him as he drinks. Hannah laughs and shakes his head.

"Goes anywhere he wants, does anything he wants," he says. "Who's gonna argue with him? People come from all over just to see him. He's still a baby, only four years old. He'll be 2,800 pounds, at least, when he's full grown. I like to come down here and sit against this fence and just look at him.

"Ain't he something?"

Something indeed. And so is John Hannah.

This article originally appeared in the August 3, 1981, volume 55, number 6 issue of Sports Illustrated. *This text was used with permission from* Sports Illustrated.

Acknowledgments

S O MANY PEOPLE have offered information, anecdotes, and memories of lessons learned the hard way, it would be impossible to list all of them in this lifetime.

Of course, God the Father and Jesus Christ head the list.

The others I will mention in no particular order of priority, and I apologize to anyone of them, who feel they have been demoted because they're not next at the top of the list, or were even left out by omission of failing memory…

- Dad, Mom, Charley, David, and Ron, who stood by me even when my ego repelled them.

- Seth and Mary Beth, two of my greatest blessings in this life.

- Major Luther T. Worsham Jr., my mentor, coach, and friend at the Baylor School in Chattanooga, Tennessee.

- Johnny Musso, No. 22, running back at Alabama who lit "the wishbone" up.

- Coach Paul "Bear" Bryant, who needs no introduction.

- Coach "Mal" Moore, former athletic director at the University of Alabama.

- Coach Chuck Fairbanks, Coach Red Miller, and Coach Jim Ringo of the Patriots, who wouldn't let me give up on myself.

- John Croyle, founder of the Big Oak Ranch in Glencoe, Alabama, who has shepherded hundreds of disadvantaged children to a productive life of faith.

- Leon Gray, the finest playing partner a lineman could ever ask for.

- Andre Tippett, a true friend and gentleman to the core.

- Numerous other old pros like Steve Grogan, Randy White, Lee Roy Jordan, Buck Buchanan, Dick Butkus, Sam "Bam" Cunningham, Russ Francis, Cullen Bryant, and countless others who were memorable (and sometimes painful) to play with or against.

- Paul Zimmerman, "Dr. Z," who authored the 1981 *Sports Illustrated* article.

- Karen Carpenter of *Sports Illustrated,* who facilitated the reprinting of the article for this project.

- Jeff Fedotin of Triumph Books, whose passion for sports and excellence in journalism worked magic with his creative and careful editing.

- Ken "Coach" Plunkett and all my other Blount County friends who couldn't care less if I was once "famous," but who still embrace me anyway as just "John," another cattle farmer trying to make a living and loving the Lord.

Afterword

As I READ what my good friend, Tom Hale, helped put to words in this book, I felt a lot of different things. At times I was happy with what was said and how it was said. At other times I felt humbled by how it puffed up my life. Sometimes I was even disturbed by what I read. There were parts of my life, which I care not to remember. But I realize my story is always a matter of interpretation. Although we speak the same language, each of us hears not only with our ears, but also with the personalized memories and experiences of our past. So, whether my story is interpreted through my eyes, Tom's eyes, the editor's eyes, or your own eyes, my hope is that through all the entertaining anecdotes, the football stories, and even the personal drama, a clear picture is revealed. That picture is both a map and a blueprint of how Yahweh, God the Holy Spirit was faithful and remains so in finishing the good work, which He started in me so many years ago.

This story is about a son of Adam. Like his father, I also wanted to be like God. I wanted to plan my own life and receive all the accolades to achieve purpose and meaning in my life. The only problem with those plans is that they didn't work. Each step of the way I asked God to bless my plans. He was faithful to my request but not in the way I intended. With each step I took, He held me by my right hand and allowed me to understand that. He is the creator, and I am the created. He shows me how to truly live a life with purpose and meaning by being obedient to His agenda. Like Paul, I had scales on my eyes, but those scales took a much longer time to fall before I could really see. There are times when I realize that I still have a few scales left, but gradually they are being removed as I follow my God, who desires a close, personal, and intimate relationship with me.

Yes, I am a son of Adam, but I am also an adopted son of Yahweh. My goal of this book was to reveal my mistakes and misunderstandings of being a Christian to other sons and daughters of Adam in the hope that you will learn the call to become a follower of Christ. In doing so, we might become like Him and bring Him the glory. He is the Creator, the adopter, the provider, and our salvation.

As you read my story, the theme is the same as that in the bible. In the beginning God created a perfect world, but mankind decided that they wanted to run things their way. As a result the perfect creation became a place and a people in ruin, but there is a solution. God has overcome, and the perfect creation is being and will be renewed. Like Abraham, I believed God, and it was credited as righteousness. Like the people of Israel, I was given the law but was found lacking in keeping it. Now I am part of Jesus' discipleship training course. I am learning that humility and dependence on God are the key principles to my growth. That's why my story is not about me but all about Him.

—John Hannah

"And you shall be fishers of Men"

-Matthew 4:19

Sources

Books

The Holy Bible Contemporary English Version, American Bible Society

Inside Pro Football Hal Higdon, Tempo Books 1968

Bear Bryant, CEO Richard Truman, Cliff Road Books 2006

Paper Lion George Plimpton, Pocket Books 1966

God's Game Plan FCA, Tyndale House Publishers, Inc. 1996

Spiritual Disciplines Handbook A.A. Calhoun, Intervarsity Press 2005

Deep Coaching R. Howe-Murphy, Enneagram Press 2007

Leadership David H. White, Rivendell Book Factory

Periodicals

"John Hannah Doesn't Fiddle Around" *Sports Illustrated*, August 3, 1981

Websites

www.nfl.com/player/johnhannah/2515751

www.espn.go.com/blog/sec/tag/_/name/johnhannah

www.prideofthetide.com/hof_hannah.htm

www.profootballhof.com/hof/member

www.rolltide.com/sports/m-footbl/archive

www.secsportsfan.com/john-hannah-biography